Hello.
Sit down.
What can I turn you into?
Do you have a favorite animal?
A favorite color?
Do you want to be something dangerous or spooky?
Something beautiful?
How about an exotic face from somewhere
around the world?

Or can I surprise you?

Now, tilt your head up a little, close your eyes and relax.
Close your eyes gently, like you're sleeping.
You don't need to scrunch them up or hide your lips.
None of this can hurt you.
Just relax. It might tickle, but it won't hurt.

And don't worry.
You won't have to look like this forever.
It's not a life choice.
It all washes off with soap and water.

Transformations!

the story behind the painted faces

text and art by

Christopher Agostino

book design by

Christa Agostino

*Dedicated to
my Mom and Dad,
who raised me
to be adventurous,
and to my wife and partner,
Lorraine, who shares
the adventure today.*

For information about the
Transformation! Facepainting company
and Christopher Agostino's stage presentation,
"The Transformation! Show," please go to:

www.agostinoarts.com

Book design by Christa Agostino
www.gmgarts.com

Published by Kryolan GmbH
Papierstr. 10, D-13409, Berlin

Printed in Singapore by Hock Cheong Printing

ISBN: 3-935946-13-9

Part of being human is to dream of being more. Our imagination is boundless, brought to life on our skin through our art. Our skin is the edge of who we are, where we touch the world.

Our art is the mark of our humanity. All human cultures, all of our ancestors, have used art to change the way we look—to create an identity.

This is the art of transformation.

table of contents

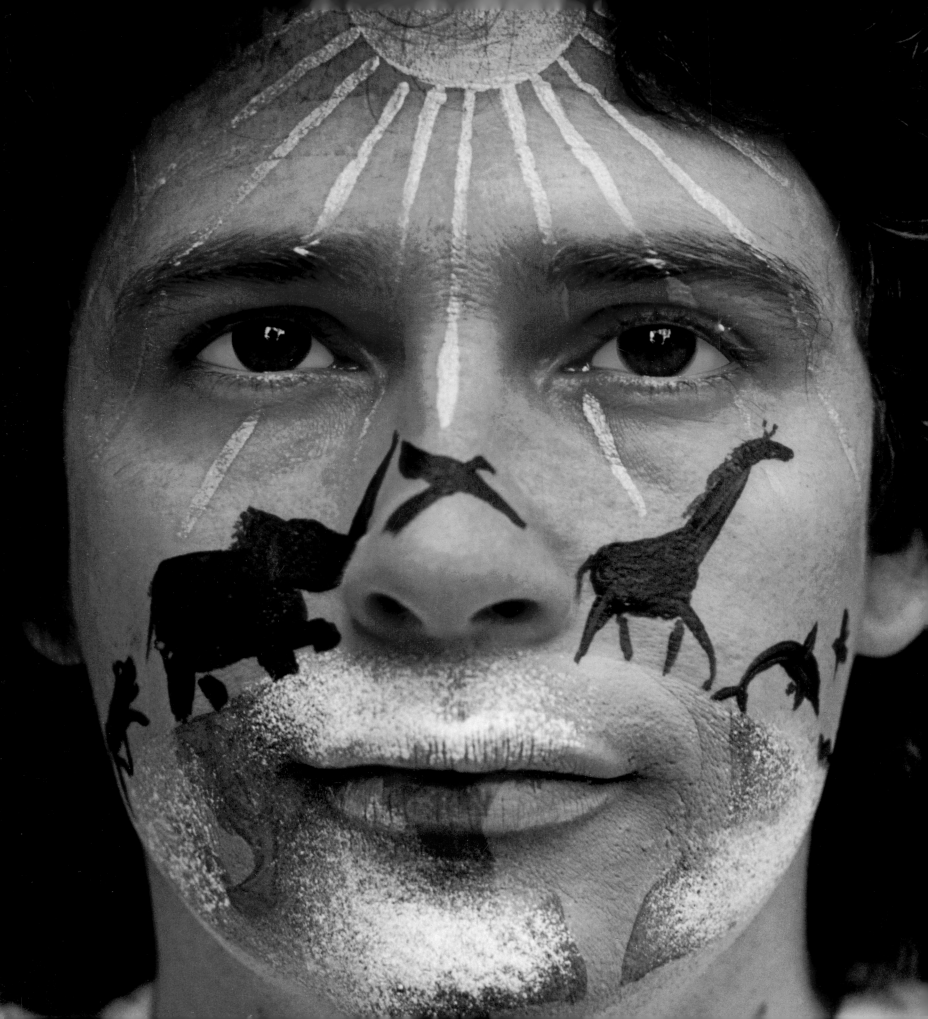

From the Beginning

We were our own first works of art. That is a profound way for a facepainter to view what he does: it was here from the very beginning. We humans painted on ourselves before we ever began to decorate the world around us.

Transforming ourselves is the fundamental human art. We take control of ourselves—we differentiate ourselves from being merely animals—when we mark ourselves. We prove that we are aware of the effect we can have on the world when we transform ourselves. It is part of being human.

Face and body art are universal. Every culture uses makeup, body art, masks or costumes to change human appearance. The reasons for the transformations in different cultures are as varied as the images they create. In traditional cultures, tattoo and scarification can mark an individual's place in society and his or her accomplishments. Those marks can signify a change in status such as an initiation completed or a marriage. Face and body painting is more transient and can convey a wide range of meanings, from ritual and celebratory to the purely aesthetic. Facepainting can disguise the wearer and allow an individual to create a new identity. Theatrical makeup and masks allow performers to become anything, even living gods that bring a mythical world to life in a physical form. In tribal rituals gods and spirits are brought to life by masked dancers so bizarrely disguised that they are unrecognizable as human. The possibilities for transformation are as limitless as our imaginations.

This is the way I approach a face when I paint it. I can do anything. The person I paint can become anything. There is an endless wealth of ideas from thousands of years of human history. There are the thousands of faces I have painted. And there is the face before me. Each face is very new and very old.

To present facepainting to the public as an art you have to take it seriously. Like a painter working on canvas you need to refine both your craft and your understanding of the art.

My art has led me on an exploration of the world history of masks, makeup and body decoration, searching for imagery and inspiration in books and the incredible museums of New York City. As fun as facepainting is on its own, learning and thinking about masks has made it an adventure. The painted faces of the Chinese Opera or Japanese Kabuki Theater; the face and body decorations of indigenous people living today in Papua New Guinea and the Amazon; the faces of Plains Indians as recorded in the paintings of George Catlin; the incredible photographs of the painted bodies of the Southeast Nuba in Africa—these are the masterpieces of the art of facepainting. I am a student of these images. They educate and inspire me, especially as I re-create them on the faces I paint.

The faces presented here are not the authentic photographs from other lands or images and drawings from other times that are the treasures you can find in books and museums. These are my painted faces. These are my view of the world of face and mask art, through the lens of my own artistic sensibilities and limitations. These are my lessons learned.

Most of the photographs in this book are of my own work on regular people painted along the way, either as part of my stage shows on the history of facepainting or at public events and private parties. There are lots of photographs here, about as many as I and a team of my artists would paint during a weekend event. Facepainting as an entertainment presents a unique opportunity for an artist to be productive. We fill events with painted faces. I like to make each face different, both to make my work more exciting for the spectators and to keep pushing myself to try new designs. There are so many different ways to paint a face.

This book is not a treatise on body arts and the cultures that practice it. Whether on stage or in this book, to speak of tribal and cultural sources is to speak in broad generalities at best. Mine is an artist's approach to subjects best explained by ethnologists and anthropologists. The complexity of so-called primitive art can never be revealed in a few words or images, nor can they represent traditions that have continued for thousands of years. All the bits and pieces of information here are filtered through my own interests and my love of a good story.

This photo was taken in 1992 at the annual St. Francis Day Fair for the Blessing of the Animals at the Cathedral of St. John the Divine in New York City. This was the first time I had painted this design on myself. It became a signature face for me which I used for many years to open my facepainting/storytelling show. The photo is by Danny Gosnell, one of our artists.

For every face has its story. It may be the story of its cultural origins that informs the design each time I paint it. It may be the story of what I have learned by attempting a face from far off lands, whether the design succeeds for me or not. It may be a memory from the first time I tried a new design. Finding and sharing those stories is one of the great unexpected pleasures of my having made a career out of painting faces.

There is a responsibility inherent in using the arts and truths of other cultures as I do. To paint a face means something to me. It means something to change a person's identity, even for a few hours. Even at a fancy party in our modern world it is part of a most ancient tradition.

A facepainter is an artist who has to ask for the permission of the canvas. When people let me paint their faces I am encouraged—especially by those who ask me to be creative or to surprise them.

Turning people into art reminds me of what we are all capable of becoming. Bringing the world to life on people's faces reminds us of the family of humanity we all belong to. The more faces I see, the more they convince me that we are all one people. Looking out through every face I paint are a pair of beautiful eyes.

In deciding to write this book, I had to ask myself if I could present my work without apology. Who am I to offer you my facepainting and call it art? Who am I to present my inauthentic renditions of images foreign to me as a representation of the profound and sacred art of the people they come from?

My only answer is that this is what I do.

My theatrical mentor, Sigfrido Aguilar, teaches that no matter the text or subject, the only story an artist can tell is his personal story. As often as I return for inspiration to the books I cherish and their images from around the world, any wisdom I have gained from them is evident only on the faces I have painted. Each face we paint is a comment on the faces that came before it and a reaching towards what can come next.

This is a record of my personal journey from face to face and the inspirations that have guided me. I offer it as an encouragement to other facepainting artists on their own unique journey.

Before we ever painted on a cave wall, we painted on ourselves.

It's a line I've used ever since the book *The Painted Body* by Michel Thévoz (1984) introduced me to the idea that painting ourselves was the first human art. He states that it is the fundamental human art: "...there is no body but the painted body, and no painting but body painting."

With images and analysis of mask, face and body art from all times and places in human culture, Thévoz's book helped me to see the range of possibilities for a painted face, and more, it led me to thinking about why I paint faces and how to put meaning into the faces I paint.

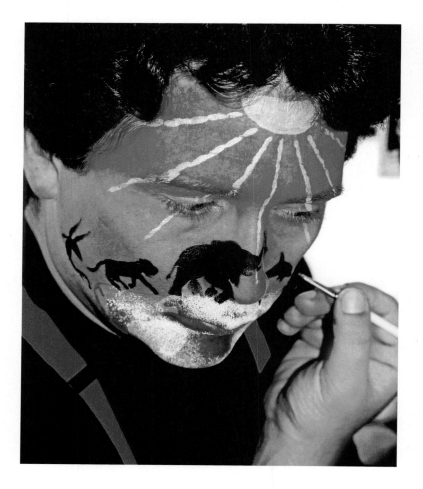

In my desire to revisit that initial impulse to paint ourselves, I collect images of cave wall paintings and other ancient art. Cave paintings bring animals to life in naturalistic and stylized imagery that use the outcroppings and shapes of the rock walls, in much the same way body artists use the contours of the human form. Much of this prehistoric art

From the earliest surviving art imagery, found on rock walls and in caves, I glean ideas for faces like red hand prints, animals in outline form and multiple animals layering and obscuring each other. Human figures in cave art exhibit signs of transformation: markings that suggest body art and animal elements which suggest masks or mythic transfigurations, like this horned dancing figure from a prehistoric rock painting in Algeria.

From the Beginning 3

depicts human/animal transformations associated with the shamanist beliefs that scholars describe as part of the foundation of early human cultures.

To apply the term "primitive art" to this art of our ancestors, or of traditional people today, reveals the limitations of our own ethnocentric bias within Western culture. In the introduction to his survey of African art, Frank Willett states that "the oldest art we know, the most primitive in its strictest time sense...is highly sophisticated. All art is sophisticated; if it were not sophisticated it would not be art, but merely a felicitous accident." Upon seeing the 17,000 year old paintings on the cave walls at Lascaux, Picasso is said to have spoken for all artists when he exclaimed, "we have learned nothing!"

In traditional cultures the artist is not an individual struggling to express his or her personal view. The artist is an integral component of the social and spiritual life of the community. Their art is not meant to be judged on pure aesthetics or "for art's sake." The symbolic content, the meaning, is the driving force behind the form, especially in ritual or ceremonial art. The true measure of the quality or "sophistication" of traditional art is the subjective response it evokes in the members within that tradition. When art is applied to the human form through mask and body painting, it leads to the ultimate subjective experience for the wearer—it allows him to be transformed. More important than how a painted face looks is how that face makes the wearer feel.

Chauvet Lions Watching

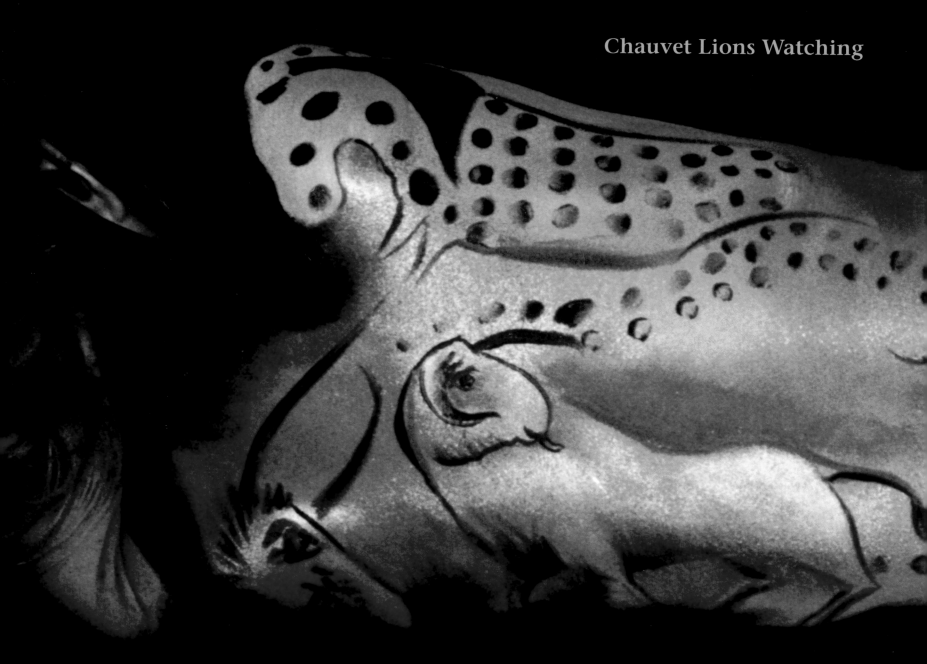

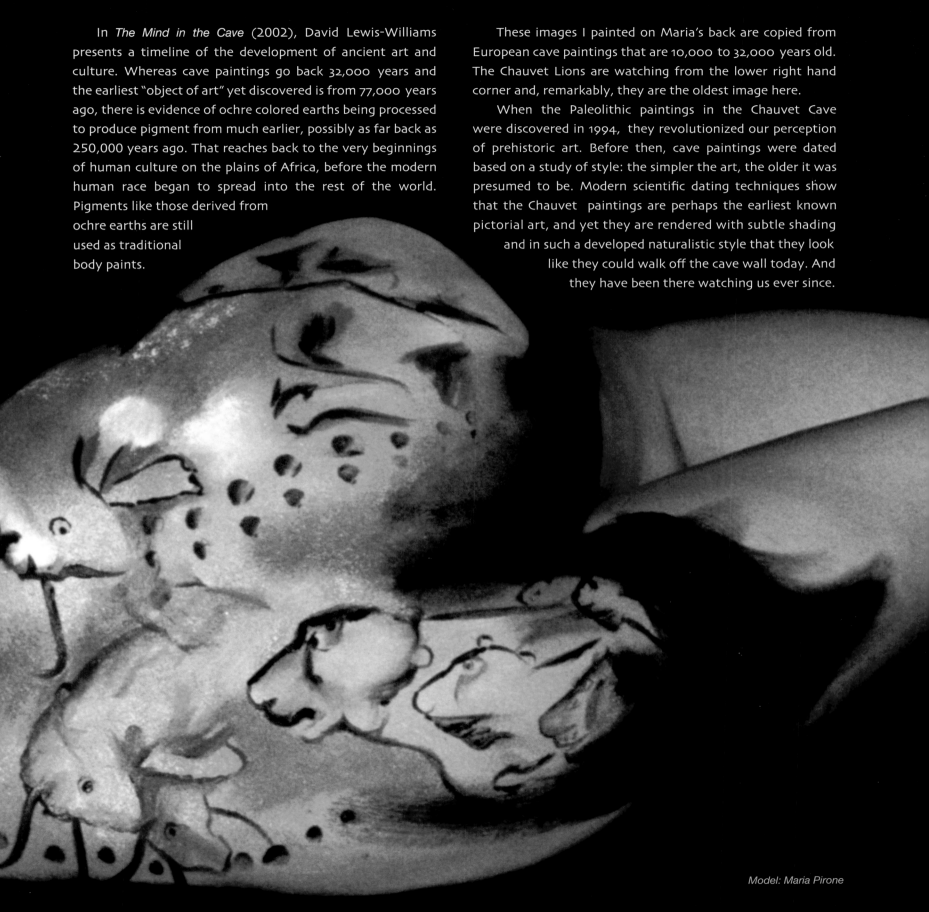

In *The Mind in the Cave* (2002), David Lewis-Williams presents a timeline of the development of ancient art and culture. Whereas cave paintings go back 32,000 years and the earliest "object of art" yet discovered is from 77,000 years ago, there is evidence of ochre colored earths being processed to produce pigment from much earlier, possibly as far back as 250,000 years ago. That reaches back to the very beginnings of human culture on the plains of Africa, before the modern human race began to spread into the rest of the world. Pigments like those derived from ochre earths are still used as traditional body paints.

These images I painted on Maria's back are copied from European cave paintings that are 10,000 to 32,000 years old. The Chauvet Lions are watching from the lower right hand corner and, remarkably, they are the oldest image here.

When the Paleolithic paintings in the Chauvet Cave were discovered in 1994, they revolutionized our perception of prehistoric art. Before then, cave paintings were dated based on a study of style: the simpler the art, the older it was presumed to be. Modern scientific dating techniques show that the Chauvet paintings are perhaps the earliest known pictorial art, and yet they are rendered with subtle shading and in such a developed naturalistic style that they look like they could walk off the cave wall today. And they have been there watching us ever since.

Model: Maria Pirone

Art Wolfe went to a Singsing celebration at Mt. Hagen on Papua New Guinea to take pictures for his 1997 book *Tribes* and saw 70 tribes participating, with only a few hundred foreigners in attendance. In a time when so much tribal art is created only for tourists, it was "most definitely a tribal event."

Before Art Wolfe, Malcolm Kirk made several visits to Papua New Guinea to create a gallery of extraordinary photographs. In the preface to *Tribes*, Art Wolfe writes, "I am forever indebted to Malcolm Kirk, whose *Man As Art* is a stunning record of New Guinea's highland tribes..."

I am greatly indebted to photographers such as these who have gone around the world to capture images of these ephemeral arts. Between Malcolm Kirk's and Art Wolfe's photographs there is such a variety of designs that they encourage a facepainter to take chances with just what you can do with the human face. Here are examples of traditional Papua New Guinea designs they have recorded as re-created on the faces of people I paint.

Face by Lorraine

1 Rain Forest Faces & Tribal Basics

Approaching tribal art as a source for faces to paint comes with one drawback: the faces you paint never look as good as the originals. As practised by tribal cultures, from the past and surviving into the present, this fundamental human art is at its zenith. Tribal body arts completely disguise and transform the human form.

When you use the faces from Papua New Guinea or the Amazon Rain Forest as inspiration, you need to have a perspective about what you are really able to understand from them. The primary lessons such cultural examples can teach a facepainter are within the designs themselves, for no tribal art carries its full meaning when removed from its culture. To look at their body art from a facepainter's perspective is to try to figure out how the design works and what parts of it you can use. Traditional designs can be models for accurate reproductions and examples of a style with which to invent your own designs. You learn something by trying to paint a face like someone who does it as part of their way of life.

Beyond the images of people from other cultures, there is the information you can find about rituals and celebrations, the varying techniques employed in their body arts and the meanings behind specific imagery. I love to learn such stories as vehicles for adding depth to my approach to the face, but there is a limit to how much you can understand of the personal arts of people in other times and places. Whether you understand it or not, you can study tribal art as you'd study any art. The people who create it and wear it are artists from whom a face and body painter can learn.

In his preface to *Man As Art*, Malcolm Kirk presents his perspective on the desire of anthropologists to give us explanations for tribal body art: "The tribespeople seem to accept self-decoration for what it is: a tradition handed down by their ancestors that is an elemental part of their lives. They feel no need to elaborate on it verbally, at least not with the kind of analytical detachment we value… [In Western culture] we seek to codify art as though we are uncomfortable with our intuitive appraisal of it." Within tribal or "primitive" societies, arts such as ceremonial body decoration have a subjective, experiential function for the practitioner and we need to use our intuition as well as our reason in our desire to understand it. As stated in one Papua New Guinea artist's explanation for the decorations of his fellow clansmen: "We look at them and we are pleased."

It is ironic that from a modern point of view, tribal body art is an indication of the savage or primitive—for the primal function of traditional body art is as the mark of civilization. Surrounded by Nature, tribal people assert their identity as humans by marking themselves with symbols that represent the mythology and social structure of their culture. By taking control of their body and identity, they proclaim their control of their place in the world. To paint themselves, to transform themselves, is to demonstrate the self-awareness that separates them from the animals.

Traditional people living today within the omnipotent presence of the Amazon Rain Forest proclaim the separation between forest and human society with a profound body art in which the wearers create their social identity through symbolic colors and geometric markings. Most Amazon Indians paint themselves every day. The color red may represent the power of an animal. Black slash marks across the eyes might signify a bird's wings. Regarding the atrist's belief in the power of makeup to transfer supernatural and animal attributes, Karl Gröning states that "with decorated skin he is capable of anything."

In the Amazon, Art Wolfe photographed a Mayoruna matriarch who wore red achiote dye over her eyes, a bluish tattoo around her mouth and palm spines sticking from her nose as "whiskers" signifying the puma, a symbol for strength. She said she needed strength because she was a new mother —and maybe, I imagine, because the photographers were in the village that day.

Tribal body art is more than just adornment or disguise, it is a visual language undecipherable outside the culture. It is the mark of identity for an individual, declaring both mem-

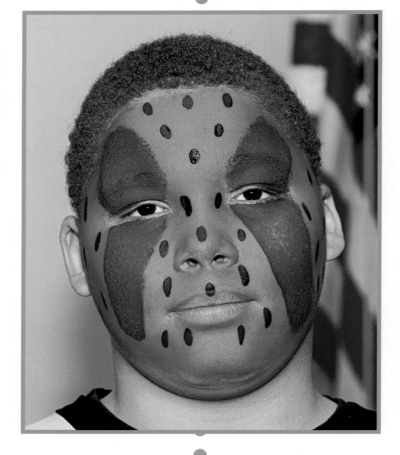

bership within the community and status as an individual. Within animist beliefs, the power of transformational make-up to disguise the wearer's true physical and spiritual identity to outsiders offers protection in a forest full of spirits—malevolent and otherwise—to be conciliated. In ceremonial use, fantastic self-adornment projects the mythic, idealized image of the individual's identity transcending the struggles of the everyday world. There may be specific designs for rituals and initiations which reinforce the social compacts of the culture by symbolically marking them on the flesh of its members. As the Caduveo Indians say: "An unpainted body is a stupid body."

Other than that excellent promotional quote for a face-painting display, what can you gain from exploring the body art of Amazon Indians? The designs, methods and philosophies of people such as the Kayapo and Yanomamö can be inspiration for a modern facepainter as well. My appreciation of the art we practice expands with each attempt I make to understand it through the eyes of another culture. It informs the faces I paint. In the following chapters on world cultures I have included examples of the designs we've painted and, especially, those faces I look at as touchstones for the lessons learned. To read about them and look at photos only takes you so far. You have to paint faces like these to really discover what they can teach you.

In the tropics, extensive bodypainting serves a practical function as well. It helps to protect the skin. One bright red dye used throughout South America is made from achiote (or annatto) seeds, which is a natural bug repellent. I was first introduced to achiote in another context entirely, as a spice I got in Mexico which stains your fingers red when you use it to barbecue chicken.

"Skin-painting puts the whole person on display, both as an individual and a member of his community. The community agrees upon the pattern, color and function of the bodypainting and its interpretation, but the execution leaves scope for the individual to show himself as such... and this individual execution opens out into the realm of art."
— Karl Gröning, on the Alto Xingú cultures of the Amazon

I'm not sure if you can change the world by painting it one face at a time, but if you are going to try, you certainly will need help. Over the years I have been fortunate to gather a company of artists who care about this art and appreciate the opportunity to do it in the same adventurous way that I do. At *Transformation! Facepainting*, we do all sorts of events, from birthday parties to festivals, and we paint people in all sorts of different ways. A part of our company repertoire is to bring cultural masks and makeup designs onto some of the faces we paint and, at times, to entire events.

We bring traditional faces into modern events both to expand our own understanding and to elevate the public's appreciation of the art of facepainting. To give ourselves these opportunities for exploration we create special cultural themes for some of our public events for clients such as the Wildlife Conservation Society headquartered at the world-famous Bronx Zoo.

For our first "Rain Forest Faces" weekend at the Bronx Zoo, we used a set of reference images of Amazon faces and devised these guidelines: *start by dividing the face with bands or bold shapes, in just one or two colors and skin; add lines and geometric designs over the base colors to create meaning; no recognizable imagery like cat's eyes or butterfly's wings; no blends.* (Try it.)

We can't learn all the authentic visual codes of the different tribes so we have to invent our own symbolic meanings for lines and colors. Sometimes we restrict our palette to traditional colors, sometimes the range is more modern but the number per face remains limited. We'll re-create some of the authentic faces we find to learn from them and get in a groove—but the goal is for the artists to explore their own creativity within the style.

Painting like this is as much of an adventure for the public as for the artists. So we tell the folks waiting what to expect: that we will be painting in an unusual style and that they will be surprised by the way they look. For a tribal theme like "Rain Forest," we will ask them to choose an attribute such as "fast" or "powerful" rather than asking what they want to be. This loosens their expectations and gives our artists room to create. The artist can interpret the request with an animal association ("fast" could be a bird, fish, deer…) or in a purely graphic way. Talking to people about their faces gives them a context, even for unusual designs. (Tell the kid you're painting that you and he are the only ones who know that his face markings are the secret sign of the anaconda).

The special events weekends at the wonderful Bronx Zoo offered ideal opportunities for creative explorations like these because people go to the zoo expecting an adventure. The first time we did Rain Forest faces in a corporate setting I was more leery. We had five artists at a large company's "Rain Forest Christmas Party" so we chose to paint in this Amazon style. The families responded well and we truly brought their theme to life. We painted as many people as we did at the next year's "Victorian Christmas" of angels and Santa Claus faces. The simplicity of the Rain Forest faces gives them an elegance that people appreciate.

In the artistic process, restrictions can bring freedom. Although initially reluctant to give up their many, many colors and familiar designs, our artists discovered real pleasure in this primal approach. They now look forward to days when we paint Rain Forest faces—free to paint with pure color, shape and line.

Here's Lorraine with a fish face she completed and a family group painted by various members of the company.

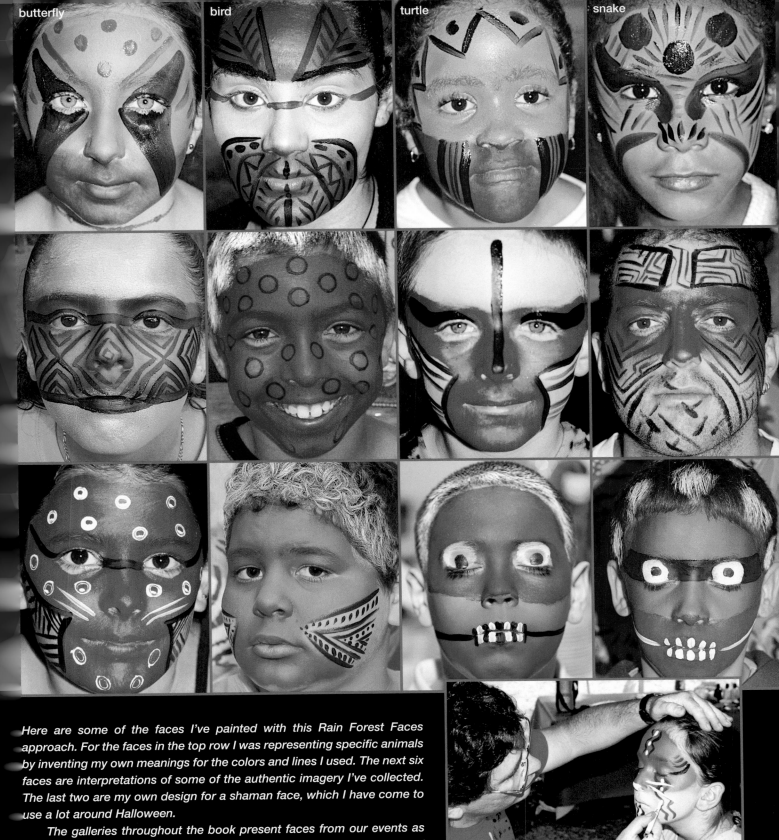

butterfly
bird
turtle
snake

Here are some of the faces I've painted with this Rain Forest Faces approach. For the faces in the top row I was representing specific animals by inventing my own meanings for the colors and lines I used. The next six faces are interpretations of some of the authentic imagery I've collected. The last two are my own design for a shaman face, which I have come to use a lot around Halloween.

The galleries throughout the book present faces from our events as examples of facepainting concepts in action. Most of the faces presented are my own, for these are the snapshots I take while working in order to record the faces that can teach me something for the next time I am

Three Key Faces

There are more than 200 tribal groups in the Amazon River area that maintain traditional cultures. The books and films that depict these people contain an endless variety of face designs. Each tribe, each family within a tribe, may have their own code of symbols for face and bodypainting. Photographs from the 1970s of the Txukahamãe of the upper Xingú include bodies covered in geometric designs of astounding intricacy, carefully painted in black dyes that last for many days. Among the Yanomamö, courting couples may use their bodies to write secret messages to each other.

While replicating and re-inventing images from such sources some faces come to encapsulate certain ideas. I take photographs of the interesting faces I paint in new styles—both the successes and the failures—and some of these become key images I can recall as a touchstone for working in that style.

The idea for this face came from the images of the Kayapo children who are painted by their mothers and kinswomen. Girls learn the art from their mothers, "the supreme painters of the village." They use a semi-permanent black dye for their personal designs, or "beautiful painting," while the upper face is covered with brilliant red paints that must be replaced daily to "energize the intelligence of the individual," according to Art Wolfe. My rendition of the cheek design is much simpler than the geometric line patterns of the tattoo-like original. The simplicity of this face is what I like. It looks nice on this girl. Without having any imagery or meaning at all, it's an attractive design.

This face is a failure with a lesson. The Conibo, Shipibo and Stetebo cover their bodies, clothes, houses and everything with delicate rectilinear patterns. As explained in the "Body Art: Marks of Identity" exhibit at the Museum of Natural History (1999), they believe the universe was once covered in such designs. On ritual occasions they will sing tunes by reading the patterns of the lines. It's not a face style you can successfully paint in a few minutes at an event, so I never tried a full face like this again, but I retain and reuse the idea of the interconnected lines to create areas of pattern—and I love that idea about singing the design of someone's face.

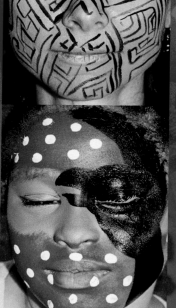

The third time we did a Rain Forest weekend at the Bronx Zoo, I was looking for ways to expand the Amazon approach beyond the traditional by adding imagery. For this face I thought of the black marks on the eyes to signify "bird" and substituted an iconic image of a parrot instead. It's Amazon Pop. This kind of experimenting leads to what we think of as creating modern masks—designs which may have an underlying traditional concept but which look good without any context.

Wildly Colorful Tribal Faces from Papua New Guinea

"Transformed by paint and plummage...they hover on that mysterious border separating the familiar from the obscure." — Malcolm Kirk

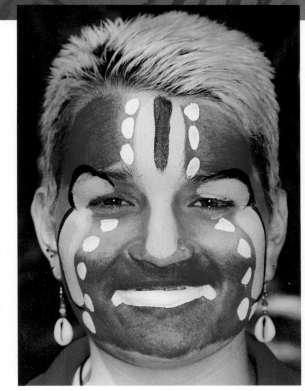

Before delving into faces from the Amazon, I had seen and imitated the elaborate face and body decorations from Papua New Guinea. The most striking examples use brilliant colors in an array of designs that appear as nonrepresentational art to an outsider. These faces helped open my mind to a wider understanding of what a successful design could be. No imagery and no fancy line work. Just wildly colorful. As I continue to paint my own versions of these "abstract tribal art" faces today, I will ask people, "Is it ok if I make you VERY colorful?"

The very colorful face on this page is one of the first truly tribal designs I painted on a guest at a corporate event. As it wasn't an animal, clown or anything recognizable, I thought at the time that the woman who let me paint it was brave to wear it. Since then I've learned that people can think it's cool to look like someone from somewhere else in the world.

Anthropologist Andrew Strathern has written extensively on Papua New Guinea body art styles, which vary widely between tribes within the general culture. They decorate themselves primarily for gift-giving celebrations that bring different tribes together. It is truly a transformational art, with face and bodypainting in combination with costuming and fantastic headdresses that completely alter the human appearance. Good decorations elevate the status of the tribesmen, but it can bring very bad fortune if you are able to recognize the dancer.

His interviews with tribal artists present a unique view from within their culture. Asked the reason for their extensive decoration, one artist, Wömndi, explains that "we men and women, both sexes, we have to stick at our work all the time, it is hard...we keep on it, we [work] in the gardens and bush, hidden from view, and so when we cook pigs...or give pigs away...we want people from other places to come and look at us."

"In Melpa [Mt. Hagen area] usage, particular designs executed on part of the face have conventional names, but the overall design does not. It is the colors themselves that carry the load of meaning, together with the stress on making recognition of men as difficult as possible."

— Andrew Strathern

The elaborate body decorations in the Mt. Hagen cultures are so complete that the individual is unrecognizable, yet this is not an attempt to achieve the traditional role of a ritual mask to allow the wearer to assume a new identity for the purpose of the ritual. Rather, the dancers wear the decorations to *represent themselves in heightened form.* Expanding your self image beyond your hard daily life is a theme for celebrations in other tribal cultures, such as the Karo of Africa (and in our own as well as we transform ourselves to go out at night or to a fancy party). It is another way for us to take control of our human identity through self-transformation.

There also is a running discussion throughout Strathern's interviews as to whether the beautiful birds of paradise of the surrounding forest are the inspiration for the body art and dancing. Whereas Ongka describes specific movements in relation to meaning (swaying relates to the dodging of arrows and other moves imitate the mating dance of male birds), Wömndi explains how all the movements are designed to make their headdresses and aprons look more attractive as they dance. In his general analysis of traditional tribal arts, Franz Boas states that underlying forms remain stabile (both within and across cultures), and that meanings change and evolve as applied to the existing forms. So the face which originated just as an attractive design may come to be seen as a bird of paradise through the eyes of a later artist (or vice versa). Artists, tribal or otherwise, will adjust and evolve formal designs for aesthetic reasons as well as their symbolic content.

Both artists agreed that the birds of paradise stay hidden until their plumes are

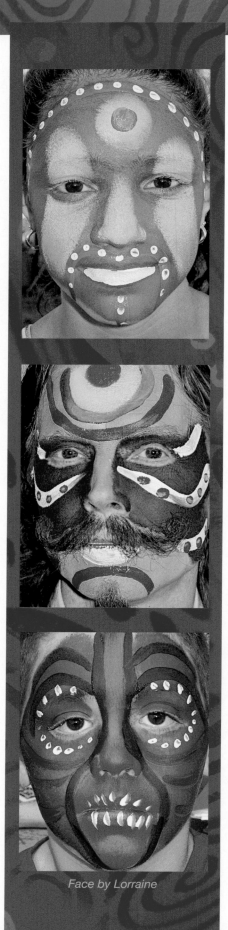

Face by Lorraine

fully grown. It is only when they are at their most spectacular that they go to a display spot and dance.

Faces like these seem so alien to us, the bizarre traditions of far away cultures. Even an attractively painted face may initially evoke a feeling of "disturbing strangeness," to use Freud's terminology—a reaction to "the return of what we have driven back" as we have moved from the tribe to modern culture.

So what happens when you paint such faces on people at events?

I have found that the use of obviously tribal imagery generates a sense of wonder and interest on the part of viewers in a way that even the most sophisticated rendering of the familiar animal and superhero designs cannot. In our approach to facepainting as an interactive art intended to transform events as well as individuals, there is a great value to making faces that are fascinating and which engage the viewer as they wonder what it is. The beautiful colors of the Papua New Guinea styles make them an ideal face to add interest to an event, whether in re-creations of traditional designs or in our re-inventions as in the three examples on this page.

As explained by Andrew Strathern, both the concept of the person and the use of makeup is perceived very differently in Western society from the way they are in New Guinea. In the West, only women wear makeup, for in our culture they are objects of desire and required to make themselves attractive every day. In New Guinea culture both men and women wear makeup, but only for celebration and ritual separate from their daily personas. For them the idea of anyone to wear it every day and for men to never wear it at all—that is bizarre.

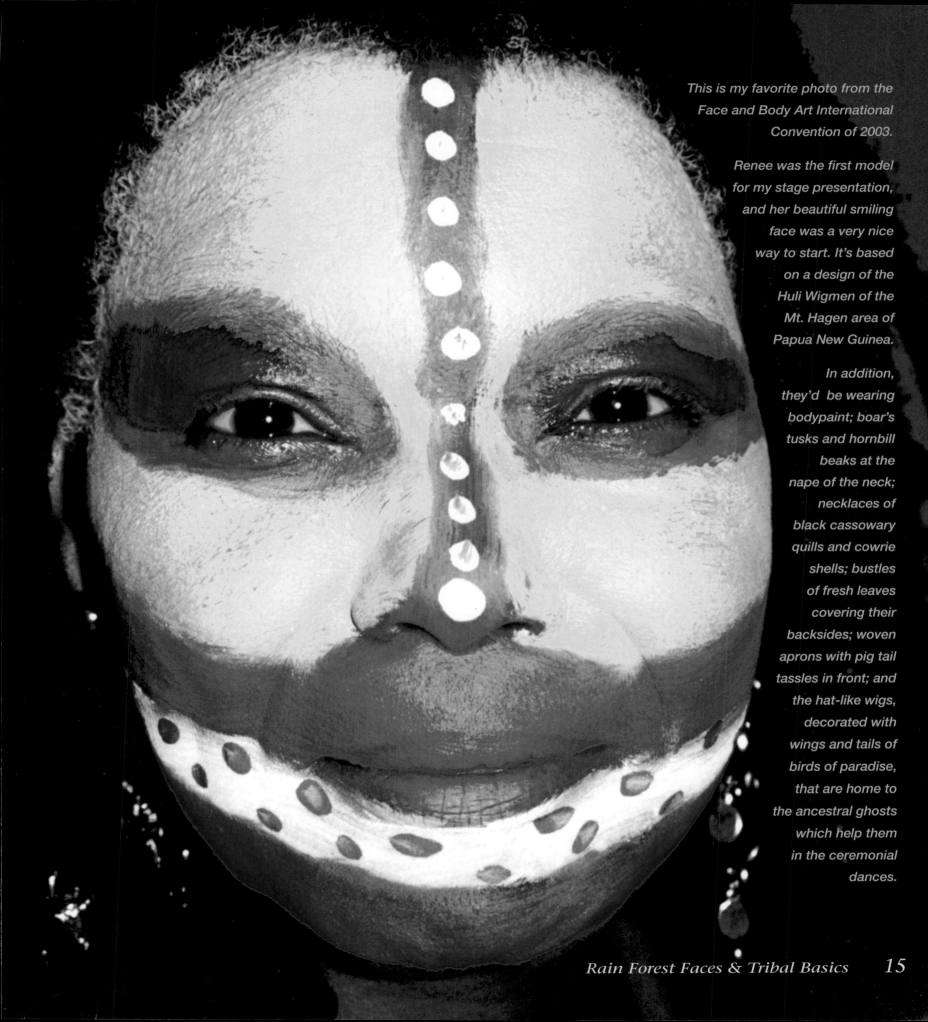

This is my favorite photo from the Face and Body Art International Convention of 2003.

Renee was the first model for my stage presentation, and her beautiful smiling face was a very nice way to start. It's based on a design of the Huli Wigmen of the Mt. Hagen area of Papua New Guinea.

In addition, they'd be wearing bodypaint; boar's tusks and hornbill beaks at the nape of the neck; necklaces of black cassowary quills and cowrie shells; bustles of fresh leaves covering their backsides; woven aprons with pig tail tassles in front; and the hat-like wigs, decorated with wings and tails of birds of paradise, that are home to the ancestral ghosts which help them in the ceremonial dances.

Rain Forest Faces & Tribal Basics 15

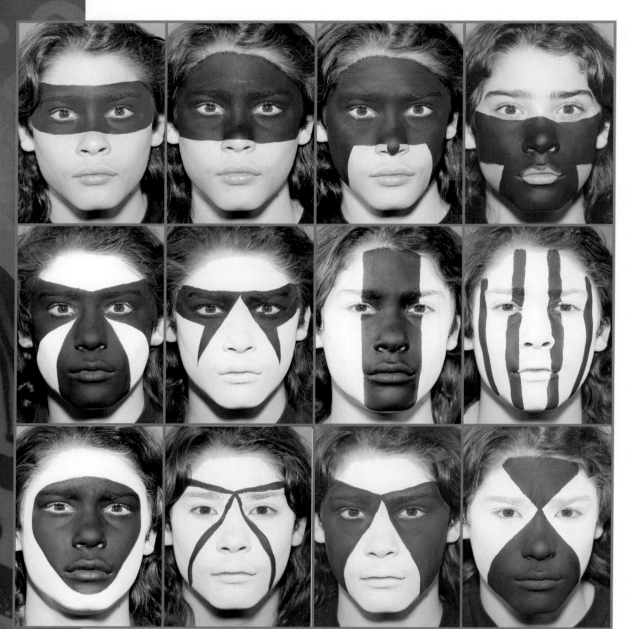

Can I even say that there is a universal tribal approach to a painted face?

While preparing for a summer of African-themed facepainting at the Bronx Zoo, our artist Jennifer Wade found a set of sketches at the public library labeled "Basic Tribal Designs (Nuba)" in the book *Nuba Personal Art* by James C. Faris. Analytical sketches like these provide cheat sheets for a tribal approach.

They illustrate what I see as the first step to painting a tribal face: divide the face into areas of color with bars, stripes or strong shapes like triangles. The quickest way to alter a human face is to put a hard line on it. Human faces have no inherent hard lines or edges, so lines or strong geometric shapes immediately make the face "non-human" and ready to become "other."

They disguise the face. They change the shape of the face. They turn the face into a mask. Just as in the approach of any modern makeup artist, the designs center around the wearer's eyes. The first goal of transformational makeup is to disguise the wearer. The second is to create another identity. I believe that by placing patterns to bring attention to the eyes, you give wearers control over their new identity.

I believe that by placing patterns to bring attention to the eyes, you give wearers control over their new identity.

You can make up your own geometric divisions of the face or you can try traditional patterns like those above —re-created here in black and white on the face of my son Jeremy. The first four are from Amazon examples. The next eight are from those basic symmetrical designs of the Southeast Nuba of Sudan, Africa. (See Chapter 4 for the incredible asymmetrical Nuba face art.) Notice how these designs affect the appearance of his eyes. And think of all the different things you can turn designs like these into.

Tribal Approach to an Animal Face

As an example of how we might take tribal concepts out of a specific cultural context and use them for something like the animal faces we paint on any gig, here are a few snakes. For each face I followed a general "tribal approach" formula which expands on the guidelines for the Rain Forest Faces.

Begin by creating a background that transforms and disguises the face by dividing it into areas of color using horizontal or vertical stripes, and/or strong geometric shapes; choose the background colors for symbolic content (like red, black and white for a dangerous snake) or to complement the clothes, coloring and eyes of the person you're painting. Over that background, add significant lines and symbols to represent the animal (such as fangs, forked tongue or snake eyes). Finally, add decorative elements or linework to unify the face as a complete design.

For these first two examples, I created a background with geometric divisions based on the triangle. For one, I was thinking of bright Papua New Guinea coloration and the second follows one of the basic Nuba patterns from the facing page. Then I turned them into snakes by adding a graphic representation of fangs and eyes.

For the three below, I divided the face with stripes and added black line work to indicate "snake." One is in a line style loosely inspired by Polynesian and Maori face patterns. On the others I used two versions of simple iconic representations of a snake. This approach leads to endless successful variations for the same face. The use of strong colors in an interesting pattern for a background makes almost anything you put on top look good. It also allows for some incredibly quick designs, especially for animal faces. It's not just the simplicity of the designs that lets you paint fast, the formula lets you paint creatively without having to think too much about each face. When I'm working quickly I'll start dividing the face with colors to make a background while I'm thinking about what signs to use to turn the person into their animal.

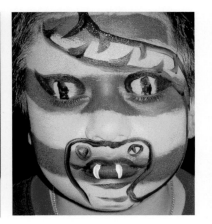

This re-creation of a sketch of an Amazon shaman's face design illustrates a key. According to the text, this was the pattern worn by a medicine man named Cobroti and these lines gave him the "strength of a jungle snake for a dance ritual, so that he could get in touch with the dead." It's a meaning that is indecipherable to an outsider like me from just looking at these lines—there is no pictorial representation here at all—and that gives me some courage to invent my own symbolic meanings for my linework. What is important is the meaning you can bring to the face as you paint it, and how the painted face makes the wearer feel and affects the people viewing it.

17

TRIBAL TATTOO

For a working facepainter, the first association for "tribal" is probably "tattoo." Tattoo artists working in California in the 1970s are credited with re-inventing Polynesian designs into the tribal tattoo style that remains popular. It's an echo of an earlier episode in which the Polynesian tattoos on sailors returning with Captain Cook and other explorers in the late 1700s sparked a re-emergence of the tattoo in Europe. Imitating a tribal tattoo is a popular request at parties today, and makeup works for the strong black lines of this style, as in the bodypaint example here. Though I don't feel that a bodypainter's ultimate achievement is to imitate them, there are many tattoo books in my library for ideas and inspirations.

The natives of the Marquesa Islands were the most extensively tattooed of the Polynesians, with designs running from head to foot. *"Adorning the World: Art of the Marquesa Islands"* (Metropolitan Museum of Art, 2005) displayed masks, sculptures, ritual objects and everyday utensils decorated with the same extensive geometric patterns they put on their bodies. Recorded examples indicate that tattoo patterns would change at times for no apparent reason. It was the act of being tattooed, not the specific designs, that transformed the individual.

Traditionally, the permanence of tattoos make them markers for personal achievements that are equally permanent, such as membership in a group, social status, coming of age, marriage and such. Bodypainting may be used to indicate the *transition* into such social states, but its effect is temporary—which is also true at parties.

"As to the tattowing, it is done very curiously in spiral and other figures; and in many places indented into their skins which looks like carving, though at a distance it appears as if it had been only smeared with a black paint...The tattowing is peculiar to the principal men among them."
— Sydney Parkinson on Maori tattooing in 1769

Tattoos can afford to be subtle or petit because they are always present. Bodypainting is so temporary it needs to be more bold. When I bodypaint at a party I want my work to stand out and be seen, so what's the point of putting a tiny butterfly on someone's ankle? When painting in a tattoo style I use color and imagery with my black line work to give it a greater impact as a painting. As in our approach to tribal faces, I will also invent symbols and patterns to generate meaning and give my tribal-esque body art a point of interest.

From authentic tribal tattoo there are visual lessons that apply to any bodypainting style, such as the use of skin as negative space and the black ink as positive space. There is also a wealth of line styles and, especially, the use of motifs: line patterns such as zig-zags or spirals that are repeated to create patterns and unify designs.

"Moko"
is the name
for the incredibly
elaborate spiral
patterns of the facial
tattoo practiced by the
Maori of New Zealand.
For a Maori man, his moko
was his identity, a record both
of his lineage and the deeds he had
achieved in life. This face pattern is my
reproduction from a sketch "reproduced
from life" by H. G. Robley in his book
"Maori Tattooing."

Maori Moko

The intricacy of Maori tattoo is such that in facepainting like it, each line you paint may represent two or three fine tattoo lines. This is especially remarkable because their method was more akin to scarification than other tattoo techniques. The lines were incised into the skin with a chisel-like implement before the dye was applied. In photographs from the 1800s, the faces of fully tattooed men have the appearance of carvings.

Master tattoo artists would also carve the moko patterns into wooden sculptures as representations of ancestors and important personages. These carvings survive as authentic examples of moko which has not been re-interpreted by European artists in their sketches. Examples also survive on preserved heads. Some of these are on the heads of fallen warriors, for it was an act of respect to take the head of the vanquished, but many surviving designs were inscribed on heads after death and sold as objects to the tourist trade.

This is a reproduction of H. G. Robley's sketch from life of a moko "showing good nose-marking" and the face it inspired as painted on Miguel.

Above is a sketch of the moko in a wood carving from 1842 that is a self-portrait of master carver Raharuhi Rukopo. The moko patterns in such carvings from the 1800s exhibit a complexity that must be greatly simplified for painting a face at an event.

On a trip to England in 1826, a Maori named Te Pehi Kupe re-created his moko in pen and ink on paper, explaining the significance of each part of the patterns: "Every line, both on his face and on other parts of his body, was firmly registered on his memory. The portrait of his moko was drawn by him without the aid of a mirror."

The extensive and fascinating story of Te Pehi Kupe is included among the researched accounts, direct observations, personal recollections and sketches from life published in the book *Maori Tattooing* in 1896 by H. G. Robley as his attempt to establish a record of an art that was "fast vanishing." It is a sentiment behind many of the books, photographs and art that I learn from today.

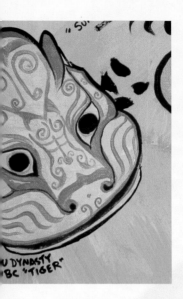

The signature spiral of the Maori moko is found throughout world art. It is one of many design patterns that appear to be universal motifs. In the 1960s, Andreas Lommel, Director of the Munich Museum of Ethnology, put together a survey of prehistoric and primitive art to explain that the prevalence of the "spiral motif" in world art is evidence of the spread of cultural ideas through ancient trade. He presents a chain of objects moving across time and cultural regions that use the spiral, including this bronze tiger head from the Chou Dynasty of ancient China with a pattern much like moko.

I love a good story. However, explanations like this which so neatly connect the few ancient dots we have make me wonder what other views we'd get from all the dots that are missing.

It's possible that the prevalence of certain symbolic images throughout the world is because we all share an underlying human culture from a very early time. Some symbolic art can be traced back as far as 30,000 years and modern genetic research suggests that there was once a single human tribe from which we are all descendants. Although it is impossible to make accurate historical determinations for the meaning of symbols from thousands of years ago, or the interconnections of the cultures that used them, some researchers search for ancient meanings by talking to the modern tribal people who produce similar artifacts. At the least it does seem that there are some concerns and beliefs that are a universal part of the human experience.

As an explanation for the development in different areas of similar design styles, Franz Boas makes a great argument in his classic book *Primitive Art* that many motifs arise as a by-product of the techniques of production. Two cultures, for example, that use a similar tool for wood carving will develop similar designs utilizing the patterns that tool makes. Along with ancient origins and cultural exchange, this may help explain the universal spiral.

The Maori provide some evidence for the role of tools in determining designs. The fine line spiral tattooing that is emblematic of moko only became prevalent after 1835 when the introduction of iron implements from Europe allowed for such detailed designs (and moko was dying out as an institution by the turn of the century). Early examples as recorded by artists such as Sydney Parkinson, who sailed with Captain Cook in 1769, may include spirals in coarser designs or within patterns that appear to be fields of solid color instead of fine lines. One of the earliest examples appears more similar to African scarification in a crosshatch pattern—another universal motif.

As a corollary to this theory that designs derive from techniques, Franz Boas goes on to say that "the same form may be given different meanings—form is constant, the interpretation is variable." We apply meaning to the designs we create, the designs that appeal to us. This, he states, is true both from tribe to tribe, and from individual to individual who use or view the same design. (So if you find a good design, turn it into different faces).

Whereas the primary function of tribal art is to carry meaning, to represent specific ideas symbolically, he also notes that as images are repeated on different objects the symbolic forms are altered to fit the object —"the attempt at decoration was much more important than the attempt at interpretation." In other words, whatever the cultural significance of their creations, artists want their work to look good. Signs and symbols become decorative motifs, and the good looking ones become universal.

In the Sepik area cultures of Papua New Guinea, spiral patterns on masks and facepainting are also marks of an individual's identity in much the same way as among the Maori. In life an individual has the exclusive right to the facepainting pattern they wear. Masks of clan forefathers and ancestors must exactly re-create the patterns they wore in life. "It is believed that only when the painting is finished will the carving be filled with the power of the cultural heroes or ancestors."
—Karl Gröning

THE USE OF DECORATIVE MOTIFS

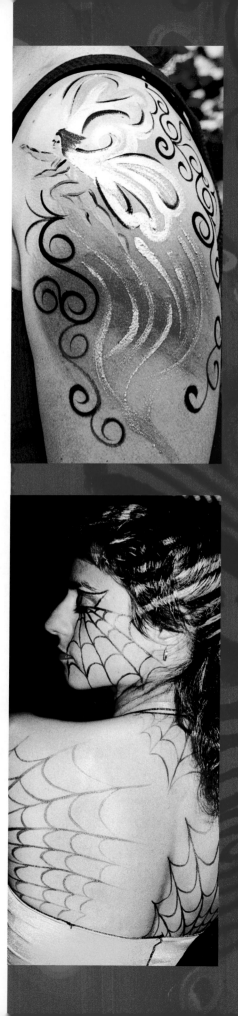

The spiral works for me, too. Once you get the wrist twirl down it's easy to apply and works well over the curves of the face. From little curlicues to make an eye design more exciting to a graphic line motif for sun rays or dragon's fire. The use of line motifs is a way to add style. You can control the style by the linework you use. Whereas a zig-zag motif might seem more formal, for me the spiral means "fancy."

To develop your own favorite motifs, find a decorative linework that you can do comfortably, quickly. Then see how many different ways you can use it.

From tribal artifacts and world bodyart you can find spots, stripes, crosshatch lines, zig-zags, checkerboards, triangles and all sorts of simplified symbols to use as basic motif. Linework can have some pictorial role or it can be purely decorative. Surround a lion face with spirals to represent the mane and bring the face into the hair. Or turn a lion face into a mask by framing it with crosshatched lines and a ring of color. Look for an element within the image that you can repeat (like a spiderweb) or take an element and move it around (as in taking some spots from the angelfish to make the background.)

On the faces throughout the book you can find examples of design motifs used to add complexity to a face in a simple way.

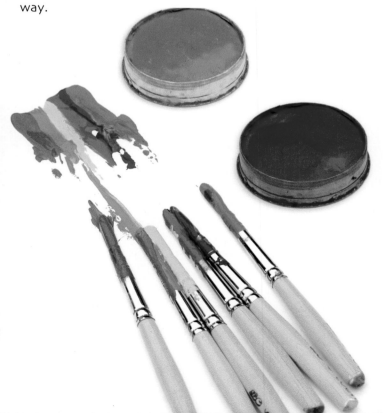

The spiral also works nicely on the surfaces of ceramic vessels, as in these dessert plates. Many of my face and body motifs naturally transfer to designs on clay, and then sometimes back again in new ways. If you work in another art or craft, bring those designs into your facepainting.

The impetus for my making our dinnerware came from a unique look into the life of a Mangbetu village of Northern Zaire as represented in an exhibit called "*African Reflections*" (1990). In the exhibit, the Museum of Natural History displayed all of the household objects collected from a single expedition to the village in the early 1900s. Everything was a work of art, from their house poles to their eating utensils. Their lives were surrounded by art.

The Mangbetu people were works of art as well, as they regularly painted themselves using a dye made from the gardenia plant. The black linework designs were applied freehand or with stamps and roulettes, to be replaced every few days as they wore off. The uniqueness of the designs was prized, which may explain why the designs shown in that exhibit look different from the examples of Mangbetu body art I have seen from other sources.

In Michel Thevóz's underlying hypothesis that all art began with body art, there is a primal explanation for why designs we find attractive are so well suited to the human form: the one universal constant in pictorial art is objects painted in a symmetry that follows the morphology of the body. *"It is as if the artists of the most diverse tribes and people had all proceeded by transferring onto the wall of the hut, the side of the box, the surface of the vase, or whatever the object being painted, a composition originally conceived as a face or body decoration."*

The Eagle In Human Form

2 American Indian Imagery
animal totems & iconography

As the audience comes in for my show at schools I give them something to watch by painting a few volunteers on stage. Whatever I am painting, there are kids that call out, "He's turning them into Indians!" It's the first connotation in an American kid's mind for a painted face.

This romantic notion of the "painted Indian" dates back, through text books and Hollywood movies, to the descriptions of the European conquerors and colonizers of North America. The image we have of native cultures is filtered through the bias of their observers and, generally, such observations dwell on the things which seem most spectacular or outrageous to the eyes of the outsider. Thus, Native Americans became "redskins" to the Europeans because of their body painting, even though it was probably "only for rituals, war parties and special occasions that the Indians dressed in magnificent costumes and painted themselves."

When I do school programs about American Indian folktales and mask arts I remind the students that this idea of the painted Native American is just as true of all natives everywhere—including all of our ancestors. The same desire to say something about ourselves through our appearance remains with us today. Just as traditional people decorated themselves for ritual and celebration, we gussy ourselves up for weddings and parties. I put my kids in their best clothes for school picture day just as chiefs wore their finest for George Catlin's portrait sessions in the 1800s. The totemic image of a bear claw on their clothes has today become the

Nike swoosh (though without the depth of meaning). We still want to project an idealized image of ourselves by the symbols we wear.

Generally in traditional cultures, masks are used in rituals and body arts have a more social or celebratory function, and, generally, the same is true in North America. Masked figures such as the Hopi Kachinas or the transformation masks of the Pacific Northwest Coast cultures allow the mythological to come to life in the real world, just as other masks do in African and Asian cultures.

Masks survive to form an objective record, something the more ephemeral body decorations can't do. There is limited information about American Indian body arts before the contact with Europeans forever changed their culture, or about how Indians might have decorated themselves in their daily lives. Face and body painting achieved its greatest significance amongst the Plains Indians as an essential part of their social structure, testifying to an individual's achievements in hunting and battle—"a face without decoration was a disgrace."

There are some commonalities to the many North American cultures but there are also great differences from tribe to tribe in the style, use and meaning of traditional body decoration which make that mental image of the painted Indian much too narrow. And it is a living tradition, visible in the incredible masks and body arts of contemporary Native American artists.

"For the spectator at initiation rites, the dance masks (which opened suddenly like two shutters to reveal a second face, and sometimes a third...) were proofs of the omnipresence of the supernatural and the proliferation of myths." — Claude Lévi-Strauss

Northwest Coast Masks

The interconnected Indian cultures of the northern Pacific coast of North America (Northwest Coast Indians) developed a tradition of art as great and as varied as any modern art. It is especially evident in their incredible transformation dance masks. In our modern culture we separate the spiritual and the spectacular between the cathedral and the circus. In Northwest Coast ritual arts these two traditions "reign in their primeval unity".

Franz Boas writes that in symbolic art, the actual appearance of the animal is subservient to the imagery that *signifies* the animal. A significant feature of this bear mask, for example, is the depiction of the human faces in the ears (though I don't know the story behind that one). A beaver must be represented by its two large incisors and flat paddle tail, so a mask of the beaver's face would include the tail even though that is not how a real beaver looks.

NORTHWEST COAST N. AMERICA

HEILTSUK "PERSONIFIED MAN"

NUXALK "SUN TRANSFORMATION MASK"

KWAKWAKA'WAKW "DZONOQUA"

The image can also be distorted to fit the form, so that a beaver carved in profile on the side of a bowl would have both teeth visible, in violation of the true perspective. NWC art, both ancient and contemporary, is full of examples of how animal body parts are moved, distorted and changed in size in order to fit the form of the object and to be clearly visible.

The same masks from the NWC region which Claude Lévi-Strauss wrote those lines about are still on view at the American Museum of Natural History to inspire a facepainter, along with recent exhibits of the contemporary work from that region at the Museum of Art and Design.

The anthropological analysis of their mask art by people such as Claude and his predecessor, Franz Boas, explains the NWC mask maker's reliance on symbolic design elements to communicate meaning. Their aim is not to imitate an animal in a mask, but to represent it.

Whereas the masks have a complexity that does not directly translate into facepainting designs, examples of their traditional body painting show a simplification of imagery. A single symbol, such as a hooked beak painted over one eye, could be enough to associate the wearer with their totem animal, a hawk. In the Museum of Natural History you can also find stamps for body art used to reproduce important symbols such as the eye-shape that means "eagle".

Mask images can become face designs through a more graphic approach as in the two at the top, or stories like this portrait mask re-invented to depict the Raven stealing the Sun. The bottom photo features face markings from a Haida portrait mask that is in the Museum of Natural History collection.

In his structuralist approach to masks, Claude Lévi-Strauss says that every mask is a transformation of another mask in that cultural system. To analyze any mask, one needs to place it within a total range of meanings of all masks. Visual symbols are used in the same way we use words in a language. Each word "does not contain within itself its entire meaning. [Meaning] is the result of two things: the sense included in the particular term chosen, and the senses (which have been excluded by this very choice) of all the other terms that could be substituted for it."

By approaching facepainting as a form of mask making, these concepts become tools for analyzing and inventing face designs. The goal is not to imitate but to signify—therefore the face doesn't need to look "real." You can create an animal face by using imagery or symbols to represent the animal, rather than the realistic appearance of the animal. (If it has two fangs and a forked tongue it's a snake). A mask is also defined as much by what it doesn't have as what it has. (So don't put fangs on your lizard face, or people will think it's a snake). Like a mask maker, take advantage of the shape and features of the face to move and distort the imagery so it looks good. If every face is a transformation of another face you paint it puts you on a path of continuous creativity.

Within the general NWC cultural tradition masks are not just made as objects of art by man. The archetypes of ritual masks have mythic origins in which they are discovered or are given to man by supernatural beings. To own or dance with certain masks brings wealth and prestige, and these rights are generally passed down through inheritance.

In *Down from the Shimmering Sky*, Peter Macnair describes a fundamental cosmology that underlies much of NWC mask culture, as originated in the "Returned-From-Heavens" dance series of the Heiltsuk: "ancestral beings depart this world and are transported to the heavens, from whence they return to materialize in recognizable form." In the Pacific Northwest, masks may depict these celestial/ancestral beings, and also these beings in their human form. This is articulated by the transformation masks, which might open to transform an ancestral being to inner human, as a way of bringing to life the origin myth of the mask.

According to one such legend, the Thunderbird mask of the 'Nam-gis people originated when the bird flew out of the heavens to help a man. Then it transformed to human form and sent its Thunderbird headdress and cape back into the sky. The mask representing this myth may be worn covering the face completely to depict the celestial Thunderbird or on the forehead, revealing the dancer's face, to become the bird in human form.

"Family Crest Mask, Kwakiutl, late 1800s...Transformation mask: this is a superb example of the lengths patron and artist will reach in order to capture the awe-inspiring theatrical qualities of a supernatural bene-factor. The great mask represents Kwikwis, the eagle of the undersea. The outer face breaks into several parts at the beak. The inner face has an explosive effect upon the viewer..."
— Edward Malin

"I wish to inform the visitors to my Gallery that, having some years since become fully convinced of the rapid decline and certain extinction of the numerous tribes of the North American Indians; and seeing also the vast importance and value which a full pictorial history of these interesting but dying people might be to future ages—I set out alone, unaided and unadvised, resolved...to rescue from oblivion so much of their primitive looks and customs as the industry and enthusiasm of one lifetime could accomplish, and set them up in a Gallery unique and imperishable...." — George Catlin, 1840

Geeorge Catlin is one of my artist heroes. In the mid-1800s he produced nearly 500 paintings of Indian culture, including 300 detailed portraits of individuals in their finest clothes and body art. It is a remarkable resource. Much of it was painted in the field on excursions into Plains Indian country and includes incredible ethnological details about their customs and appearance, including extraordinary visual records of face and bodypainting.

He was a fine portrait artist who captured the individuality of his subjects in a way that his contemporaries did not. He toured his Indian Gallery of paintings and artifacts through the United States and Europe, and also published a series of popular prints of his paintings for the general public—including the portrait of Four Bears, a chief of the Mandan, which established the iconic image of the Indian in an eagle-feather war bonnet that we all know.

His paintings are a staple of reference books about Indians and about body art, and, in 2003, the Smithsonian Institute published a catalog of his gallery with essays on his work and controversial life. In 2005 the exhibit came to the Museum of the American Indian in Manhattan and I spent several inspirational hours staring into the eyes of Buffalo Bull, Fast Dancer and the other remarkable people who remain alive today through his art.

George Catlin made a career out of portraying "the living manners, customs and character of an interesting race of people, rapidly passing away from the face of the earth," and thus is sometimes criticized as another white man exploiting a native culture.

W. Richard West, as a Cheyenne and Director of the National Museum of the American Indian, writes that Catlin's paintings say as much about him as about his subjects. He describes Catlin as an artist who genuinely cared about his subject matter operating in a time of great complexity in the interaction between the U.S. and Native Americans. He also points out that Catlin was wrong about the vanishing Indian culture: "What Catlin shows us, perhaps unwittingly, is that the 'primitive' people he had painted long ago achieved a level of cultural sophistication and aesthetic accomplishment with which we are still coming to terms, and which continues... through the work and art of the descendants of those whom Catlin painted."

"La-Dóo-Ke-A, Buffalo Bull, A Grand Pawnee Warrior"—the face design in the lower two images and on the facing page is from a remarkable portrait by George Catlin that encapsulates the use of iconography. The totem sign of the buffalo is painted on both chest and mouth, suggesting that the man's words have the power of the buffalo. The black buffalo head set against the red bodypaint is reminiscent of a buffalo silhouetted against the setting sun. Above on the right is the face design of an Iowa warrior named "Fast Dancer" who wore a handprint on his mouth, perhaps to signify that he killed an enemy in hand-to-hand combat. To wear such a sign is to make a strong statement—the Plains Indian equivalent of "talk to the hand."

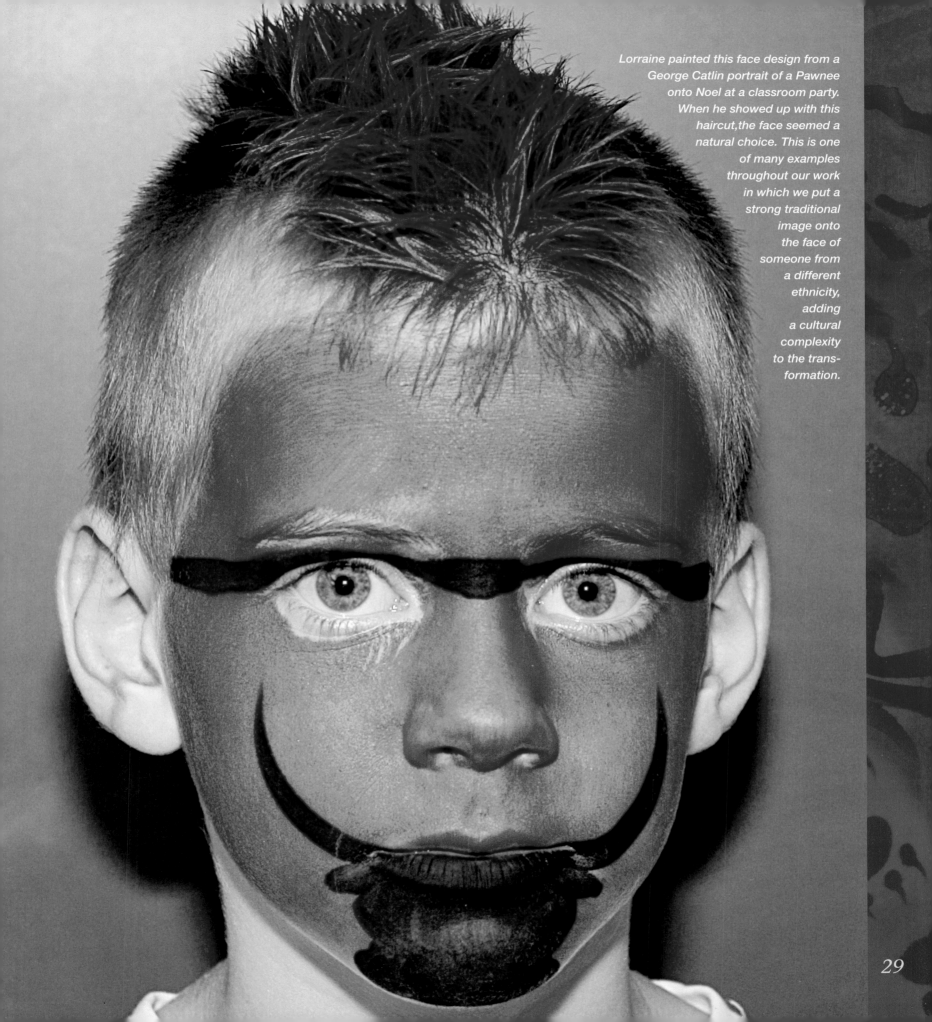

Lorraine painted this face design from a George Catlin portrait of a Pawnee onto Noel at a classroom party. When he showed up with this haircut, the face seemed a natural choice. This is one of many examples throughout our work in which we put a strong traditional image onto the face of someone from a different ethnicity, adding a cultural complexity to the transformation.

29

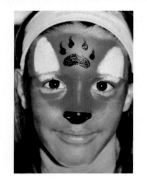

Our Animal Totems

Totemism is the single umbrella under which a very wide range of beliefs are covered. It is a term used, abused, frequently reinterpreted and too complex for a simple definition. For the Cree, the identification with one's "totem descent," is paramount. Each newborn is linked to certain ancestors and therefore to a totem animal that would be seen "as a distant relative under an obligation to help."

In a broad definition as animals used in symbolic associations, the totem concept is something observed generally throughout native cultures, as such cultures live in a codependent relationship with the natural world—a relationship we have lost in our cities.

Michel Thevóz sees this relationship as an underlying origin of body art. As humans develop culture, nature remains as "the surrounding otherness against which man must constantly reassert his existence," so the line between nature and society must be delineated, in part by body markings.

The prevalence of animal imagery in body art is because animals "represent the intermediate being between the unnameable and mankind." Becoming an animal may be a way to claim control of the instinctive being that man suppresses through culture.

The fundamental use of animal symbology by American Indians can be seen in an individual's identification with a group (such as the bear society), the use of animal artifacts or imagery (such as bear claws), and the pivotal role of animal representations in ritual dances.

In the practices of some American Indian tribes, animals function as mediators between humans and a natural world governed by supernatural forces. Among the Mandan, for example, by wearing the head and pelt and dancing like a buffalo, the hunter sought to gain empathy with the tutelary spirits that govern the buffalo and so call it to be hunted. While dancing so disguised, he still wore the bodypaint that marked him as a human and signified his status as a hunter.

The dances performed in which people became the embodiment of an animal lent credence to the belief that the bodily form was transitory, that one could transform from human to animal.

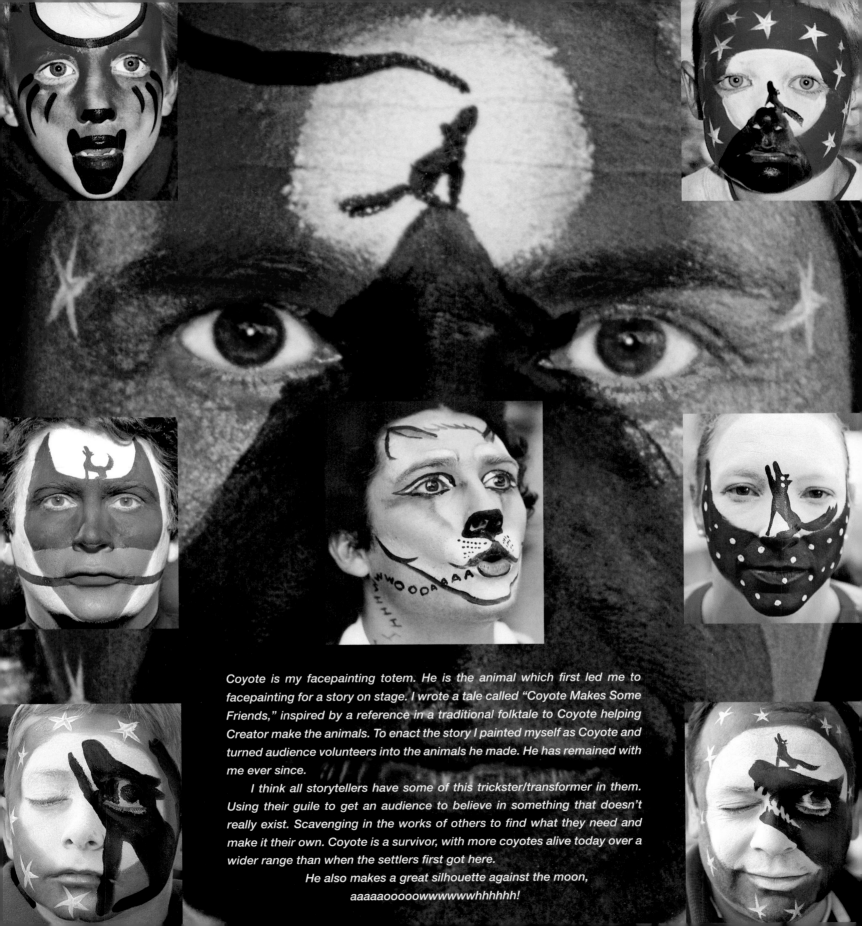

Coyote is my facepainting totem. He is the animal which first led me to facepainting for a story on stage. I wrote a tale called "Coyote Makes Some Friends," inspired by a reference in a traditional folktale to Coyote helping Creator make the animals. To enact the story I painted myself as Coyote and turned audience volunteers into the animals he made. He has remained with me ever since.

I think all storytellers have some of this trickster/transformer in them. Using their guile to get an audience to believe in something that doesn't really exist. Scavenging in the works of others to find what they need and make it their own. Coyote is a survivor, with more coyotes alive today over a wider range than when the settlers first got here.

He also makes a great silhouette against the moon, aaaaaoooooowwwwwwwhhhhhh!

Iconography & Animal Silhouettes

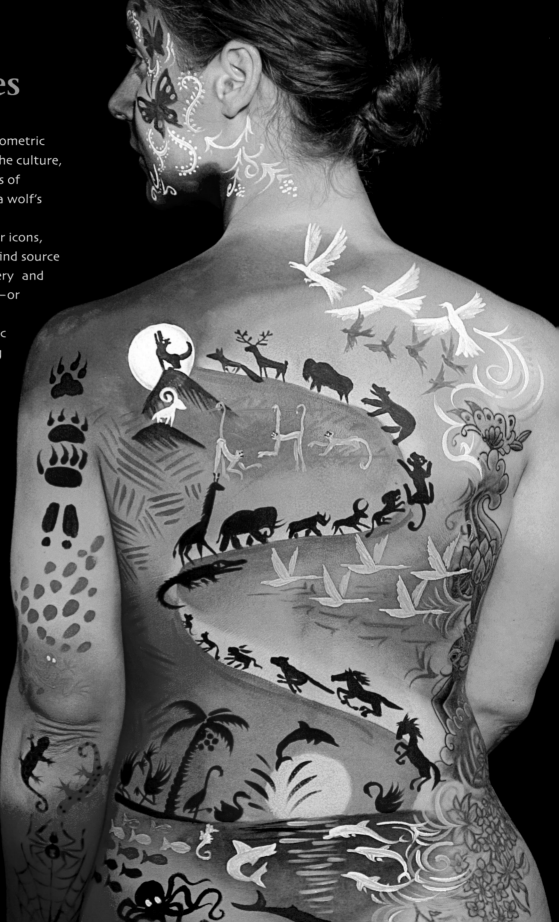

Whereas Amazon bodypainting uses codified geometric signs that are only decipherable by members of the culture, North American Indian art also includes examples of pictorial symbols we can recognize: a bear claw, a wolf's paw print, the head of a buffalo.

For a facepainter, these simplified pictures, or icons, can be used to add content to a design. You can find source images in American Indian pictographs, pottery and painted decorations on all sorts of art objects—or you can invent your own icons.

To simplify an animal down to an iconic symbol, use a design incorporating or exaggerating a significant feature of the animal (like the buffalo's head with extended horns in the Catlin portrait) or use a silhouette of the full animal's shape. Learning the silhouettes of animals is especially useful, as an animal can be recognized by its shape.

You can paint the shape of an animal in one solid color. It's an easier, faster and often more effective way to represent an animal for a face design than a full-color, detailed approach. Most often I place animal silhouettes in black against a brightly colored background, but you can also use white animals on dark backgrounds (like dolphins in a blue ocean) or make your animal shapes in colors (like sky blue geese flying across a sunset).

Once you can paint the silhouette you can add selected details to emphasize the significant features of an animal (like the teeth of a shark), or add elements for more purely decorative effects (like putting yellow spots on a black gecko). Remember that an image doesn't need to be realistic to communicate meaning. Just as the mask makers do, when you put the silhouette image onto a face, you can adjust it or distort it to better fit the features and make a better design.

The animal silhouettes that have been walking across my nose for the past fifteen years first showed up on the side of a bowl I made to commemorate my wedding with Lorraine. Later they walked around Lorraine's belly to celebrate the coming of our son. Since then they've been walking across all sorts of places.

How does an idea turn into a face? I'd done a parade of realistic animals on someone at the St. Francis Day Fair to capture the march of the animals into the cathedral. Then I saw a wonderful painted face with a black pterodactyl against a red sky, sent to me on a greeting card from England, and also an image of shadowy giraffes in an African sunset. So my animal parade became silhouettes against the sunset.

When you find something that works, use it and reuse it: *Recycle your ideas!*

"Kabuki makeup is already in itself an interpretation of the actor's own through the medium of the facial features. On stage this interpretation becomes a temporalization of makeup in collaboration with the audience. The result is a decoding of the drama traced out in the graphic designs of the painted face." — Masao Yamaguchi

3 Asian Theater gods and heroes of china, japan and india

In the traditional theater of Asia, the actor is the show. The stories are well known myths and historical epics, so everyone knows the plot. The audience is there to see the performers, their mastery of the stylized movements and voice and their otherworldy appearance in costume and makeup, as they embody legendary roles in a larger-than-life fashion. The formality and stylization of their appearance frees the performers from naturalistic expression. The actors become living special effects to present the story through codified gestures, postures and movements. As the makeup is integral to this complete transformation of the actor, Asian theater includes the most sophisticated facepainting designs in the world.

The spectacular faces of the Chinese Opera can turn performers into anything, from heroes and villains, or gods and monsters, to all sorts of clowns, animals and theatrical characters. As an actor appears on stage the color and pattern of his makeup lets the audience know his role. The makeup style of the Peking Opera has been used for 200 years and is the most well known of over three hundred regional variations. It is a vibrant art today, as in a 1991 Chendu Sichuan Opera production of "Wresting the Dragon Throne," in which the makeup of wicked Prince Yang Guang is altered throughout the play as his evil ambition possesses him. There is a wealth of inspiration and innovative ideas for a facepainter in Chinese Opera designs.

"In Japan, as in China, the theater has preserved the painted faces from ancient magic rituals in a stylized artistic form," writes Karl Gröning. The famous Kumadori makeup of the Aragoto style Kabuki—like the samurai hero design on the facing page—is not meant to be a mask to hide the actor. It is a makeup designed to capture and project the expressions of the actor in enhanced form, to externalize the inner persona of the role. Kumadori is traditionally applied by the actor with his fingers so he can feel his bone structure as he paints himself, "improvised in the hushed atmosphere of concentration that proceeds the show." It lives and moves with each facial gesture, yet it is bold enough to project the performance throughout the theater.

Throughout India, body decoration with signs and symbolic colors is practiced in all sorts of contexts: religious markings worn as signs of devotion; the Holi festival in which people color each other with powders and liquids as a renewal of friendship; the Puli Dancers bodypainted as tigers; painted elephants; and the henna patterns on hands and feet which have made it to the U.S. as a party entertainment like facepainting. Actors in the Kerala region are transformed with makeup so elaborate that it is more accurately described as living masks, becoming mythological gods and goddesses for secular performances that maintain the quality of ancient rituals.

Everything you might want to learn about facepainting can be found in the faces from Asia.

The first cultural designs that had a direct influence on what I was painting on people's faces came from the Chinese Opera. The truly classic makeup for the female role was on the cover of a magazine (*Geo*, Vol. 2, December, 1980) with photos of twenty other characters inside from a regional Chinese Opera company. Those faces became an immediate source of inspiration very different from the clowns, superheroes and KISS faces that I had been painting.

I don't think I've ever seen a more elegant and effective transformation of the shape of a human face than that design on the cover with the white on the nose and the red over the eyes blending off onto the cheek. I painted it on my facepainting partner Jenn in LA in 1983 and we used the photograph of her on the facing page as a logo image to promote our RE:FACE facepainting business.

From this face came a whole new way of looking at what I was painting on people. It embodies the idea of a painted mask. It is very beautiful and exotic and the kind of face that people respond to even when they don't know what it is—the kind of face that lets people know you're not just there for the little kids.

It is a tremendous lesson in how to achieve the maximum effect through minimal means. With three colors and very simple linework it completely transforms the face, demonstrating that it is the design, and how you place it to use the features of the face, that makes a transformation effective.

This was also the first time I'd seen the blending of colors on a face used for anything other than the naturalistic shading in standard character makeup. In these regional examples the blend was from a strong red over the eyes through soft pinks to the white of the chin,

and it makes a very powerful impression. The more traditional Peking Opera style often has a subtler blending from pink to white.

So many interesting ways to use the eyes can come from these concepts. When I moved back to New York in the mid '80s and started painting faces in the window of Unique Clothing in Greenwhich Village, I played with mixing this look into some Punk stylings to suit the current fashion, as in the two examples above. It is also a great start for fancy faces or to make a girl into an exotic princess, as in the examples to the left.

In a Chinese Opera production, this design may be worn by any or all of the female characters and for male characters as well—but I have always thought of it as the Chinese Princess. That's what I tell little girls they are becoming when I paint them like this.

I also tell them that this isn't the fairy tale princess we are used to, who sits around in a castle waiting to be rescued. The Chinese Opera tradition includes female characters who are heroes and warriors, based on legends such as those of the Warrior Maiden Mu Guiying. When I saw a touring production from China, they featured the tale of the Jade Princess. Wearing this makeup, she had two big swords and was beating up the bad guys while singing and dancing. That's a Princess!

"Suddenly a whirlwind of color blows in from stage right, quickly followed by another. Fantastic beings, made larger than life by enormous shoes and padded shoulders, leap before the audience...but the most astonishing thing about them is their faces, painted in bold and calculated designs of many colors. Everything gives the impression that some mythical creatures have taken the stage. Then one of them begins to sing." — Peter Lovrick

Red-Faced Generals and Other Painted Faces

The Chinese Opera includes a number of powerful faces that work well on men, based on some of the designs of the *jing* ("painted face") characters. The most spectacular makeups belong to these villians, supernatural beings and legendary generals such as Guan Yu, with his red makeup and long black beard. In a scenario typical of the historical operas, "The Huarong Pass" relates how General Guan Yu allows the villainous General Cao Cao to escape with his defeated army rather than watch them be slaughtered. For such courageous and honourable acts, Guan Yu was deified by later generations, so that actors today put a black mark on the cheek to show they are only a poor imitation of this general who is venerated as a god. The face above, painted at a Purim party in 2005, is the General Guan Yu design from a 1954 production in Peking.

The Shattered Face

There is no character identification beyond "the shattered face" for the sketch in *Body Decoration* of this Chinese Opera design on the right. Assymetrical makeup is unusual and something people respond to. It stands in such sharp contrast with the regularity of our facial features that the effect is unsettling. I use this design to depict a nightmare in a Chinese legend I tell and it always gets a reaction when I reveal it.

The similar design above is based on another face from the Peking Opera. In this example especially, the swirling lines give the whole design a sense of motion as if the face is still in transition.

The Clown Face

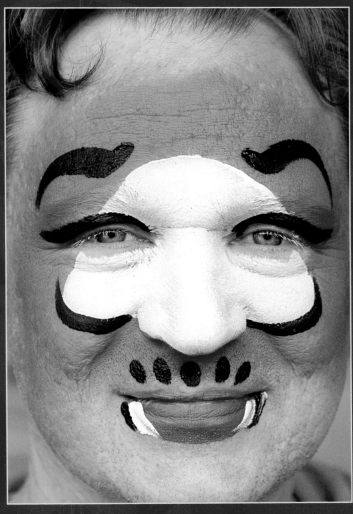

Sometimes a face design comes with its own story. The clown is identified by the distinctive white patch or triangle worn over the nose and eyes—it's the Chinese equivalent of the circus clown's red nose. It is a unique look, and by crossing the eyes with a line and effectively removing the nose with that solid white triangle, it's as complete a transformation of the shape of a face as any.

As I recall it from that *Geo* article of twenty plus years ago, the old performer who was the clown in the company gave the reporter this explanation for that mark:

An ancient clown, looking up to the heavens for guidance, saw a white bird flying far overhead, a sign of great fortune. He pointed up into the sky and called out, "Look, it's a bird!"

The bird pooped and got him right in the nose, and clowns have worn that mark ever since.

The Chinese Opera clown ("*chou*") is the character closest to the audience, using colloquial speech and bringing in improvised references to current events while exhibiting virtuosic acrobatics and physical comedy. Rich men, commoners, generals or high officials may all be portrayed as clowns, for "class or position cannot disguise clownishness for very long."

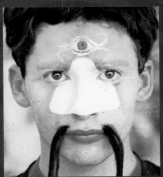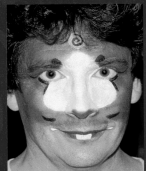

It's a face I like to wear myself on the right occasion: from Halloween in 1983 to the FABAI Banquet in 2005.

I've always investigated the faces I've found by painting them on someone, as in the photo at bottom from 1983. The four above it are recent re-creations of authentic designs, from top to bottom: Black Whirlwind, an outlaw, from a modern Peking Opera production; next, an unidentifed character, Peking Opera, 1983; these next two are from earlier eras, as depicted in a great exhibit in the Museum of Natural History—the blue one is from the Ching Dynasty of the 18th century and the red one is from the Ming Dynasty, 17th century. I painted three of the four at a cultural event where we were hired to paint Chinese Opera designs. The fourth was at a school fair the week before where I did a little practicing.

The Monkey King

"The monkey king, Sun Wukong, is a familiar and favourite character for children and grownups. He is full of energy, mischief, and fun. Any opera with the monkey king in it is sure to dazzle the audience with acrobatics and antics." — Siu Wang-Ngai and Peter Lovrick

He's a powerful warrior with a great sense of humor who can transform or trick his way out of all the misadventures he stumbles into. Everyone loves the monkey king—except for the gods, as he frequently gets the best of them. For the audience, he is a symbol of the common man who can defeat the mighty.

Sun Wukong, the monkey king, plays a key role in several Chinese Operas based on the novel *"Journey to the West."* The scenarios read like a series of action-comedies that start when he eats the peaches that grant the gods immortality because he's not invited to their banquet and then defeats the armies of the gods led by the Heavenly Warrior and his mighty clubs.

When Sun Wukong has to battle the spider spirits, he turns himself into a troup of monkies by plucking hairs from his body and blowing them into the wind. The breathtaking skills required to bring such transformations to life on stage is a hallmark of the monkey king.

The red makeup scheme is a stylization of a monkey face (perhaps a red-faced macaque?) but the color also signifies cleverness and courage. The heart shaped design narrows the face, which makes it appear smaller and helps give the illusion of a monkey mouth.

These monkey kings are modeled on the photograph of a regional actor in the 1980 *Geo Magazine* who had distinctive golden eyes painted on his eyelids. The usual Peking Opera pattern has white eyelids with a stylized eye design.

The Talking Frog

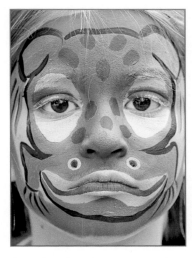

In addition to all the heroes and villians, Chinese Opera includes face designs for animals treated in very playful ways, such as the frog on the forehead in the photo on the bottom of the page, which Naoko re-created from an authentic photograph. These designs have led us into all sorts of new ideas for our own animal faces.

Danny had been facepainting with us for several years when he had the opportunity to move to China. He came back one summer and brought a book full of black and white stylized opera face designs. Several placed the mouth of an animal onto the mouth of the actor, like this rabbit face design which has a full rabbit silhouette on the face and an additional cute little rabbit face on the mouth. That face led to the leaping tiger you can find on page 116. I also adapted the idea for what has become my favorite fish face, and that helped us solve the tricky problem of how to turn people into fish for events at the NY Aquarium at Coney Island.

This wonderful frog design, from another sketch in Danny's book, shows just how much fun you can have with an animal mouth, both as a facepainter and then bringing it to life as the actor. Imagine this frog telling you a story...

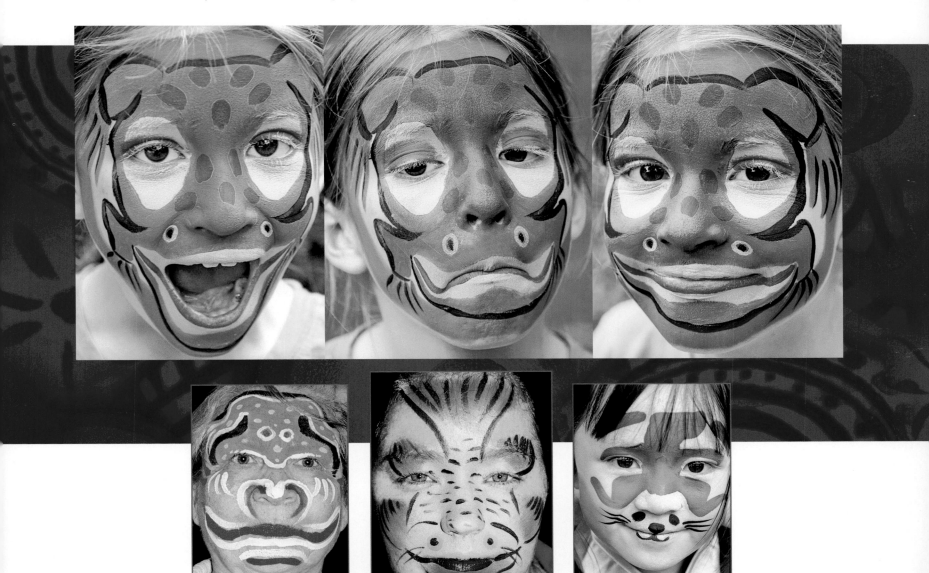

The Japanese Demon

Sometimes a face comes with a story, and sometimes a story comes with a face.
This is a tale set in a classic period of Japanese history, about one thousand years ago.

The Demon on Omi Bridge

The Governor's soldiers are hanging out together talking, and one is bragging on and on about how brave he is. Having heard enough, a fellow soldier says, "Oh yeah? Well I bet that you aren't brave enough to cross Omi Bridge." For many years no one had dared to cross the bridge in Omi provence because of the stories of a terrible demon that lived in the middle of it. No one had ever actually seen the demon or, perhaps, no one had lived to tell what they'd seen.

"I'd cross that bridge," said the braggart, "if I had a fast enough horse." "You're on," said the others, "take any of ours."

"I'd need the Governor's own horse to ride across that bridge," said the braggart, thinking this would get him out of the bet, for the Governor's horse was the fastest of all and not one meant for a common soldier. What he didn't know was that the Governor had been listening from the adjacent room, and he came in saying the soldier could use his horse, for a man must live up to his boasts however foolish they are.

The Governor and his men went the long way around the river to wait for the soldier on the other side of the bridge. Meanwhile, the soldier went down to get the horse from the stables, but first he smeared grease over the horse's back end—just in case it wasn't fast enough. He rode to the bridge and started across it as fast as that horse could go. His confidence rose as it sped across the bridge so quickly that he felt like he was flying.

Then, in the middle of the bridge, he saw a beautiful woman walking to *about the demon, he thought, and he pulled up the horse to rescue her. As he bent down to grab hold of the woman, he saw a glint of yellow in her eyes. Fearing it was the demon in disguise, he spurred the horse on and rode past. Looking back the soldier saw the demon transforming into its true form, its long arms reaching after him. The furious demon grabbed for the horse with knife-like claws—but they slid off the grease. "I'll get you next time!" yelled the demon.*

When he made it across the bridge, the Governor greeted the man as a hero and offered him the position of captain of the guards, but the soldier refused. Only he had seen the demon and it was a sight he could not forget: nine feet tall, arms seven feet long, with three claws on each hand, a blood red face with two sets of fangs and one glowing yellow eye.

He resigned his post and locked himself in his house, afraid that the demon would come after him. Whenever he closed his eyes he saw the glowing eye of the demon staring back.

The soldier was right. You should never mess with a Japanese demon. One year later, on the anniversary of his ride, his brother came to his door with news that their mother had fallen ill. His wife let the brother in and went to get them tea. Soon she heard her husband scream and call for his sword. But when she came, it was too late, for it was in truth the demon. As she watched, it bit her husband's head off. The wife raised the sword, afraid the demon would come for her, but it did not. "That is the end of that," said the Demon of Omi Bridge, and it was never seen again.

There are great examples of Japanese demon faces in prints, tattoo designs and masks such as the Namahage mask on the left, which became this face-paint design below.

The mask is a contemporary example from the Akita Prefecture, and it is worn for a traditional Lunar New Year celebration which sounds like Halloween in reverse, as young men wear the masks and visit people's houses to scare their children and admonish them to listen to their parents—or the demons will come back! The parents reward the young men with sake and food. Although frightening, Namahage are said to be gods who bring good fortune, an example of the beliefs connected to spirit worship traditions in which powerful demonic spirits can become protective when they are appeased.

The prevalence of such beliefs within the medieval Japanese culture allowed for the growth in Edo province of *"Aragato,"* the style of Kabuki theater which produced the famous makeup for its samurai hero. The origin of Kabuki and other Japanese theater in shamanic ritual and spirit worship is evident in the hero's ability to do the impossible because they have allowed themselves to be possessed by a powerful **kami** ("supernatural deity") and thus have become *hitokami* ("man-gods").

In folktales, Japanese demons come with various descriptions. Some may be red or blue faced, with fangs, horns and one, two or three eyes. In the tale of the famous samurai Raiko and his battle with the Goblin Spider, he is attacked by an army that drops out of the storm clouds, including animals that walk like men, beings with three claws and three eyes—one with eyes in its hands—and long serpents with human heads. There's a few ideas for facepainting.

The *Demon of Omi Bridge* is a tale I tell while transforming a volunteer from the audience. The tale as I found it said that the soldier "saw a red face with one amber-yellow eye as huge and round as a cushion." A folktale with its own special face included is like finding gold for a storytelling facepainter.

"In a way completely different from the realism and individualism basic to the makeup used in Western theater, Kumadori stylistically beautifies and emphasizes the stereotypical personality of a specific role. At the same time, unlike the Noh masks or the Chinese stage makeup used in Peking Opera, the Kumadori allows for greater power of expression since it closely follows the actual facial features and expressions of the actor." — *Toshiro Morita*

When you have demons running around, you need heroes to fight them. In 1673, a fourteen-year-old actor named Ichikawa-Danjuro I invented a performance and makeup style to present the "super-human actions that a righteous and courageous hero undertakes in standing up to forces of evil." This is the *suji-kuma* or "sinew pattern" worn by the samurai hero of one of the Aragato ("wild show") Kabuki dramas as it is seen today, and the red pattern expresses the positive Yang anger of the hero "with the heart of a child." His makeup is so fierce that the actor can strike a "glaring pose" to scare away evil spirits just by looking at them (which this kid on the right seems to have down pat). Other red patterns may be used for animals and comic roles. Indigo patterns represent the Yin anger that is held in until it darkens the heart and turns one to evil, and those are worn by characters such as the evil aristocrat, ghosts and demons.

Michel Thévoz writes that the influence of Japanese theater on Europe in the 1950s was to bring a sense of the sacred back to the stage: "The significant thing is that makeup thus recovered its magical function as a vehicle of the supernatural, deliberately transgressing the natural features of the human face." In my explorations of body art from tribal origins through modern cultures, I see an interesting evolution. In its original function, body art is a social act, marking the individual as a member of human culture and elevating him above his natural state. In modern cultures, transformational makeup survives in the arts where its most profound use is to take the wearers beyond their humanity so they can portray the supernatural and the super-human.

Kabuki makeup demonstrates the importance of fitting a design to an individual's features. The red stripes radiating from the center of the face are an incredible visual expression of power. Though the eyelids are left white, the eyes are framed above and beneath with black to let the actor make maximum use of his eyes.

The Kabuki Kids: from left to right. we have a hero pattern worn by Ennossuke in 1981; the Benkei-Saru-kuma ("Benkei's Monkey Pattern") said to have been designed by Ichikawa-Danjuro I; another monkey pattern; and a really cool one (but I don't know what character it is) using that Chinese Opera Princess nose trick.

Kabuki Spooky

Throughout October I find myself drawing heavily on my Asian influences for spooky faces. Why not? I think we can see it works in faces like Darth Maul and those of the professional wrestlers. The same techniques that make for powerful depictions of legendary heroes and villains can be used to bring an exotic quality into familiar Halloween characters. The eyes of the Chinese Opera Princess are particularly effective for vampires, witches and spider people. I make my Kabuki samurai more spooky by adding round glaring eyes (painted on his eyelids), in an imitation of the intense eyes they're given in Japanese prints.

Halloween is the official U.S. holiday for facepainters, as far as I'm concerned. It is the one time when we are still seen in our ancient role as the holders of the key to supernatural transformation. On Halloween in 2004 we had people lined up waiting for as long as two hours for our faces at the Bronx Zoo, and I've never experienced such a happy crowd—willing to wait as long as it took to be transformed. On that day I really felt the magic in the makeup.

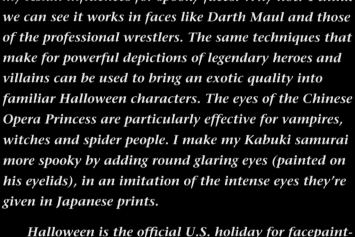

Living Gods of Kerala

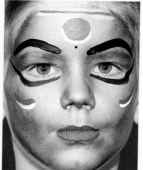

We humans want to see our gods. In many cultures, "the mask brings gods to earth" and allows a human performer in disguise to represent the unknown and unknowable. It is a primary function of masks that they can present an image so alien that it couldn't be human, as in the transformation masks of the Pacific Northwest Coast Indians and the spirit masks of certain African peoples. In the Kerala region of southern India, however, the same incredible transformation is brought about through makeup.

It can take hours of intricate face and body painting to turn a performer into the living embodiment of a god for religious festivals and performances in India. In the Kathakali and other dance theater traditions of Kerala, performers add wing-like additions, movable mouth plates and bulbous noses to their makeup to literally turn their faces into living masks to become the characters of mythological stories *("Kathas")*. By using makeup rather than a wooden mask, the performer retains the use of facial expressions and the movements of his eyes in enacting the stories. Karl Gröning states that "applying the makeup is a long, slow process that is carried out by experts while the dancer relaxes, gradually transforming himself into the strongly characterized figure he will play."

To the left are some of the faces I painted inspired by images from India. The two blue faces at the top come from images in the book *Kerala (2001)*, given to me by Niru in another example of one of my wonderful artists bringing a book back from far off lands. The first face is from a photograph of a street full of dancers depicting "Arjuna Nirittam at the Atham Festival", all of whom wore this same makeup along with elaborate headdresses and costumes.

The two faces towards the bottom of the column on the left are not authentic designs. The orange one with the dots is an example of how we might use cultural sources to bring a new look into something like a princess face. The face at the bottom is a tiger I painted at the Bronx Zoo with the Kathakali style in mind, on a Big Cat weekend when we were painting lots of tigers and I was looking for any inspiration to bring variety to such a familiar subject. It doesn't look like a real Kathakali face at all, but just thinking of that style pushed me into a new direction.

I took three practise runs before painting Christine in this facepainting design from the Theyyam Festival for the photograph on the facing page. The Theyyam is a very old form of ritual dance from north Kerala. In an example from 1985, it took three hours to paint with plant dye the intricate patterns on an actor's face that would allow him to "exercise divine power for a couple of days and nights." My design here is a combination of that one and another example.

The first time I tried it was on myself, pictured below. The other two here were painted at events, and so the linework was simplified. Until I tried it, I wasn't sure that you could paint this kind of face quickly enough to do it at an event, but you can, for even with simpler linework it looks exotic and sophisticated. And I enjoy telling people they are becoming a god or goddess as I paint them.

4 African Abstraction
ritual, celebration and pure aesthetics

The place which may be the origin of the transforming arts in all human cultures was the source of the inspiration which transformed my company in 1999. We had already been painting at the Bronx Zoo for six years, pushing our facepainting into more artistic choices than we could at the usual commercial or fee-per-face events. We would change not just what we painted but also what style we painted in to suit featured animals for special event weekends.

To promote the opening of the magnificent **Congo Gorilla Forest** exhibit in 1999, the zoo chose to feature The Harambee African Dance Company and us. We were asked to provide 10 facepainters for eight weekends. That allowed me to lead my artists past the usual animal faces into an experiential understanding of facepainting within a set cultural style.

When they asked me to paint a couple of faces for their ad campaign, I got a sneak peak at the exhibit under construction. The care taken to reproduce the look of the Congo rain forest and their inclusion of African art and masks suggested to me that our facepainting should follow suit. I decided that we would only paint the animals in the exhibit (which includes snakes, insects, hornbills, certain monkeys, gorillas and others, but no "pop" animals like lions or butterflies), and that we would work within traditional African mask and facepainting styles.

One day that summer, Miguel noticed this group of 25 people as they posed for a picture after coming out of our facepainting tent and he snapped this photo for me. With ten of us working, it would have taken only ten minutes for us collectively to have painted them all.

Research & Application

The diversity of imagery in the transformational arts of Africa is staggering. The many different cultural regions produce masks that range from the exquisitely realistic to the profoundly abstract. Body arts include every possible technique from scarification and tattooing to bodypainting with all sorts of materials in widely varying styles. The wealth of source imagery is so great that one can get lost in it. Africa. It's too big of a place, too diverse a set of ideas, to fit under one name.

In researching an area of the world to develop reference materials for an event, I might only find a few photographs which then come to represent an entire culture. Any image is limited. It is a record of one moment in time within cultures and arts that are constantly evolving. The same photographer 50 years—or even two weeks—earlier may have recorded very different images. As documented in the case of Leni Riefenstahl amongst the Nuba, the outsider who comes to record a culture also has an effect on that culture and that record. ("They soon noticed how impressed I was by their handiwork, and from then on competed for my wonder and admiration by devising new masks every day.")

We see a photograph in our *National Geographic* of a face in an exotic locale and we think, "that is how they live," when no picture can truly inform us about another person's life.

I approach these cultural images as examples of the same visual art I process in my work. I use them to learn as any artist might learn from a fellow artist—it is the art of these traditional cultures I am re-imagining and not the people who originated it.

To prepare reference sheets for my artists, I will select a few face or mask designs as visual archetypes representing different stylistic approaches. In practice at an event, we may paint some accurate renditions of these source images to find the stylistic groove and then go on from there to find our own designs.

For the Congo Summer, I collected images and sketches of African masks and body arts from books and the extensive collections in New York Museums, and asked my artists to do the same. We looked for specific designs and approaches that lent themselves to facepainting. We found ways to alter or add imagery to turn traditional designs into recognizable representations of the animals we were painting. We got images from the zoo of the animals in the exhibit, so that we could also do realistic or scenic animal faces, especially for the younger kids getting painted.

We all learned a few things that Congo Summer. Geometric and fabric designs turned out to be as effective a basis for a face as animal imagery. The designs we found on a sculpture or mask could also work for a face—though usually we had to simplify them. Black and white, or earth tones, can be as exciting as bright colors. Basically, we learned that face designs didn't need to be familiar to be good.

People were excited to be painted in these different, adventurous ways because the whole event gave them a context for it. We would tell the person we were painting that their abstract snake design is based on a four foot tall mask in the Metropolitan Museum of Art with diamond shapes over the eyes just like the Gabon Viper in the exhibit. With ten artists on per session we had the time to develop new ideas on the faces we painted and, just as importantly, to give people the story behind the face.

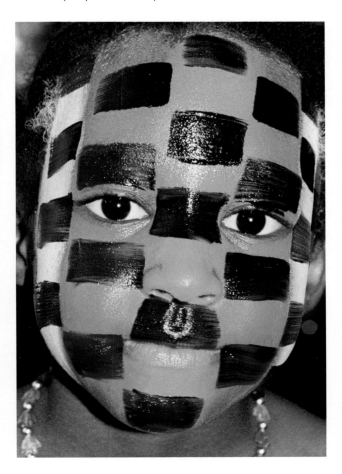

I learned something important for myself that summer. I found that I could talk to my facepainters as artists, giving them challenges, setting restrictions and criticizing when necessary. I could ask them to look at the faces they painted in the same way they might look at a canvas they painted in their studio. This was the transformation in my mind from having a company of facepainters to having a company of artists who facepaint.

Even a single image can lead to a different way to paint a face. There is one beautiful example by the Loma bodypainter Gaou Beayogui of Guinea in *Body Decoration.* According to the book, gifted artists paint girls at the time of their coming of age initiations with charcoal black patterns like "stylized plants." The body paintings "mark the change from the natural state to the realm of culture. When colors fade...the girls are regarded as adult and marriageable woman." It is an evolving tradition as these designs are also used today to decorate the walls of houses. I add colors and use the patterns on faces.

The faces I find are sources of visual inspiration that must sometimes be considered separately from their ritual context. In *African Art* I found a painted face with slashes of color delineated by white lines described as a design worn by Ngere girls in preparation for a festival after their initiation. The text reports that the carved masks of the Ngere are also very cubist in style. In appearance it's a colorful, celebratory face and I use this concept to create original, brightly colored abstract designs, even though a second, more recent source connects their facepainting tradition to a controversial ritual within that tribal culture. Because we can't always understand the reasons behind the art and practices of other cultures, I try not to judge.

African Abstraction 51

Karo Dancers

In the Omo River region of Ethiopia there are a number of cultures that practice body decoration. The Karo are perhaps the poorest, and yet they are the most colorfully decorated. As Art Wolfe writes, "In a region marked by bloody conflict and meager pastoralism, their bodies become the canvas of their self-expression." When the annual rains return, the grasses grow and life gets a little easier, so it's a time for painting yourself up and dancing in celebration. In addition to the face and body painting they create striking hair styles by weaving macrame and colored clay buns into their hair to hold feathers and beads. The elaborate transformation through body art may be a way to separate their harsh daily lives from the spirit they express in celebration.

It's an elemental style that is as basic as facepainting can get: earth tones, spots and lines. Divide the face into areas of base colors and put a pattern on top of that.

The patterns they use may symbolize or be inspired by particular animals, although apparently not in the totemic sense of acquiring animal attributes as in Amazon cultures. During the Congo events when kids asked for a leopard face I might tell them I was giving them the tribal version and paint one of these spotted Karo patterns. The following year I read that the spotted feathers of the guinea fowl were a more likely inspiration than leopards for the Karo face patterns— the guinea fowl which happened to be on exhibit at the zoo right up the path from our facepainting location that whole Congo Summer.

As simple as they are, these are attractive designs. The earth tones look good. At the start of a carnival at an upscale private school, I painted the two girls in the photograph above. People stopped to watch and remark on how interesting it was to see faces like these. It had a positive effect on the whole day's facepainting.

"On special occasions every tribe member is painted with striking designs using rusty red pulverized ochre, black charcoal, yellow mineral rock, and white chalk. First a base coat is applied to the body which is then decorated with spots to imitate the graphic feathers of the guinea fowl or the fur of a leopard. Dots or hand prints can be applied on bare skin as well."

— Art Wolfe

  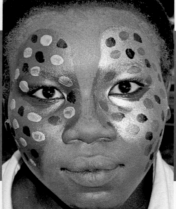  

The Surma

> "Their faces and bodies are the canvas on which African painters display their art. Decorated skin turns the body into living sculpture and elevates it to a work of art; its conscious design marks it as an expression of human civilization, which, through art, is firmly distinguished from the unformed nature that surrounds it."
>
> — Karl Gröning

In the same region as the Karo, there are the Surma people. It's a culture without much clothing and both genders use body art extensively during the three-month period of the Donga Stick Fighting tournaments between villages, when "young Surma men and women spend considerable time painting their bodies and adorning themselves to attract the opposite sex."

The best artists are male and they paint themselves both to attract women and to intimidate their opponents in the competition. The technique of the men is remarkable. They smear white chalk over their bodies and then use their wet fingertips to incise designs into it to expose the dark skin underneath. Covered from head to toe in geometric line designs, the human form indeed is transformed into "living sculpture." Carol Beckwith and Angela Fisher describe their painting tradition in *Faces from Africa* and marvel at their creativity: "Each day the Surma would return [from the river] with new designs. They were so spontaneous— painting from pleasure, using the body as canvas, oblivious to the impermanence of each day's work of art."

Although it's not a technique you can duplicate on a facepainting gig, we do use the line patterns the men create for face designs.

Beckwith and Fisher also have wonderful photographs of Surma women painting each other by a river bank, using ochre pigments in addition to the chalk. The women's designs are less elaborate and can be a direct source for faces. We have noticed that they are a type of tribal face that women at events respond to favorably and will request for themselves. Perhaps because of the gentle colors and patterns they are exotic without being too alien. They are another example of the effectiveness of ringing the face in a color, as we first gleaned from the Maasai, to create a very balanced appearance.

The Surma children also paint themselves for fun. They begin at an early age by imitating their parents, learning how to decorate themselves for the courtship rituals they will be joining as adults.

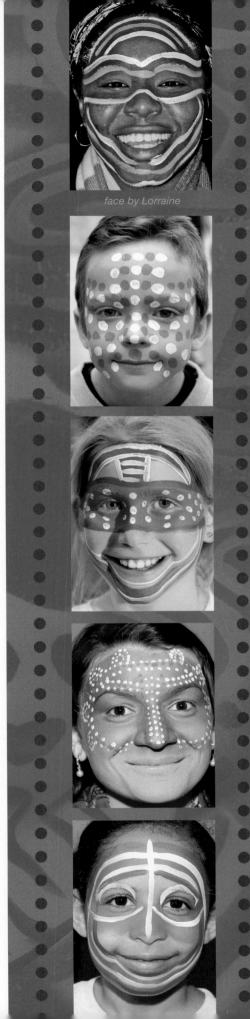

face by Lorraine

From The Maasai: A Ring of Color

The Maasai of Kenya and Tanzania are one of the most recognizable tribal groups from Africa. Many photographs feature Maasai in bright red body paint, as in the Red Dance ceremony to celebrate the warriors and those who killed "a lion armed only with their wits, their courage and their spear." Their body art traditions are determined by their age group, with the young men of the warrior (or *"moran"*) age-set wearing the most elaborate self-decoration. Some photographs show Maasai Moran in full body paintings, with intricate geometric patterns reminiscent of the Surma men.

One of the lessons I've learned from the Maasai is that I can never know the complete story of another people. Every time I think I understand their use of body art, I find another source with different information, or meet someone who's been there, or paint someone who is Maasai—and the story changes.

The culturally related Samburu people are photographed in even more extravagant body designs, including hairstyles that may take three days to coif. The Samburu Moran facepaintings include linear patterns and beaded jewelry coming in from the hair to decorate the face, as re-imagined in facepaint on the facing page.

Both cultures use the distinctive red ochre bodypaint on their necks, cheeks, foreheads and into their hair to effectively frame the face in color.

Ringing the face like that is a remarkable tool for unifying any design you put on a face. Once I began painting these faces that Congo Summer and saw what this "ring of color" approach could achieve, this technical innovation became the basis for all sorts of designs for any theme.

Framing the face in one color achieves the goal of transforming the face like a fully painted face does—which is very important to me—without covering all the skin. It's more aesthetically pleasing than painting just the forehead and cheeks of someone who doesn't want his or her "whole face" done. It can unify purely decorative elements like flowers or butterflies. It's a bold design but avoids the eyes and mouth, making it ideal for young kids' faces and for finicky "don't paint the eyes" parents. It became the leaping tiger design I put on a 3-year-old here, and that led to a series of animals-wrapped-around-the-face designs for young kids.

This is perhaps the clearest example of my belief that you can learn new approaches by imitating traditional facepainting just as a painting student learns by copying masterpieces hanging in museums. To truly learn the full lesson, however, you need to paint the face on someone. You need to feel how it's done and see what it does to the face you are painting.

Then see where it leads you.

Spirit Masks

"In body art, attention is drawn to certain parts of the body and their attractions are emphasized. With mask patterns, on the other hand, the intention is often precisely the opposite: they are meant to be remote from the mortal world and show that the beings portrayed are outside human society. Heavily stylized, so as to produce an alienating effect, they embody non-human beings such as spirits, mythical figures or animals."
— Karl Gröning

One of the primary uses of masks is to allow the wearer to impersonate a supernatural being or god, as among the Northwest Coast Indians and the traditional theater of Asia. Some of the most striking examples of such ritual and secret-society masks come from the BaSongye, Batetela, Bakuba and others from Zaire. They use strong line designs and strange shapes to make an appearance so bizarre that it couldn't possibly represent a regular human.

That is the conceptual lesson I take from these masks into facepainting: bold line patterns that make for very weird faces. These photos are examples of how I have translated this into facepainting designs. The masks themselves can't really be copied onto a face, as their shapes are anything but human.

It's not a style one would naturally use while painting faces, as we are usually working within the comfort zone of making people look good. I have learned that unusual does not always equate to unattractive. Adult men wear these designs very well. Some kids find it cool to look so different. They are also a good start for alien and monster faces.

Not surprisingly, they make for good god faces. I use an adaptation of a BaSongye design for Nyame the Sky God in my telling of a classic Ashanti story about Spider Anansi. When I reveal that face I always get an amazed

Tiger Spirit

Gorilla Spirit

reaction. As advertised, the design is so strange that the startled audience is willing to believe it's the look of a god.   The "African Genesis" exhibit at the Metropolitan Museum of Art in 2003 included some of the most beautiful masks I've ever seen presented with their cultural context. There were short films of the ceremonial uses of the masks and each mask was displayed with the mythological story it represented. The four-foot-tall snake masks with the diamonds over the eyes (which I mentioned earlier) actually seem to slither into life when worn in the dances of the Baga people of Guinea. They represent the snake spirit that guided the Baga to their home lands and dove into a river to later re-materialize as a rainbow at the river's source.

The elders of the Bwa or Bobo Oule people meet the subjects of their sacred family masks in dreams and then tell the mask makers the precise geometric patterns to use—patterns which correspond to the esoteric language of their bodypainting for initiation rites—to create "abstract masks unrelated to anything known" in the artist's senses. Their mask rituals are enacted to restore the balance between Nature and Man, with the masked figures acting "as human emissaries while remaining entities of the bush."

Behind every face there is a story.

Taking a traditional art out of its cultural context and using it for inspiration needs to be done with respect. During the Congo Summer I sometimes questioned the propriety of my being a white American painting wonderful African images, especially on the beautiful black faces they might be said to really belong to.

None of the faces I paint can really be "authentic," removed as they are from the culture that gives them meaning. They are re-imagined representations of the original sources for this art. By using cultural images, I believe we remind our public audiences of the entirety of the family of humanity.

Part of the profound beauty of a painted face is that you can't see the color of the skin beneath. My explorations into the earliest human art and cultures convince me that we all truly are one people, sharing a universal view of who we are from our origins in a fundamental human culture—which probably came out of Africa, by the way.

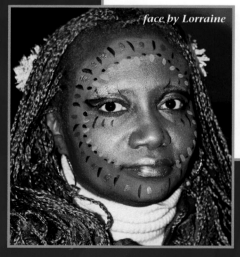

face by Lorraine

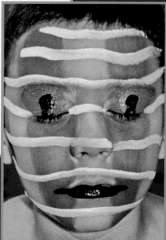

The San people (or "Bushmen") of southern Africa are thought to have one of the oldest continuous human cultures. Their rock paintings and shamanist trance dancing are considered modern remnants of the origins of art and ritual.

In 1905 Africa again became a source of inspiration for world culture as traditional sculptures and masks made their way to Paris and a whole generation of Western artists changed the way they viewed the human form and how they depicted it in art. As Frank Willet states, when masks from Africa were seen by Picasso and Matisse, "the revolution of twentieth-century art was underway."

What I learned from my work with African influences showed up on this model above for the cover of the *Abercrombie & Fitch Spring Quaterly 2000*.

This face is a re-creation from a photograph by Leni Riefenstahl. The abstract ostrich (or antelope?) eye design also made it's way into pop culture when Frank Miller put it on his corrupt police lieutenant in the graphic novel and subsequent movie, Sin City.

The Fantastic Art of the Southeast Nuba

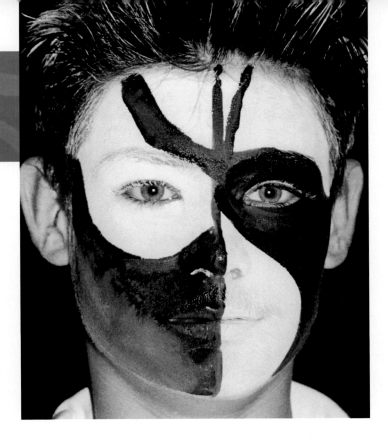

"What fascinated me more than all else was the painting on the men's faces...Sometimes figurative but often quite abstract and serving aesthetic rather than ritual purposes, their drawings displayed a command of all the canons of art, whether they painted themselves symmetrically or asymmetrically, and whether with ornaments, lines or stylized figures, the effect was always harmonious. Their use of form and color sprang from the very fount of art."

— Leni Riefenstahl

The most profound and inspirational images I've seen of tribal body art are from the Southeast Nuba of Sudan. The photographs are unique and stunning. Fully painted bodies in a seemingly endless variety of designs. There's both animal imagery and abstract non-representational decorations in whites, ochres and deep blacks. Especially startling are the asymmetrical paintings that somehow achieve a remarkable sense of balance.

Although many of the 100 or so Nuba groups use body arts, none practiced it like these 2,500 people living in a remote location among the three villages of Kau, Nyaro and Fungor. It seems that in their isolation they evolved the kind of ceremonial body art seen among other tribal groups (like the Karo and the Surma) into a complex social art that depended more on pure aesthetics than on ritual meanings. Several factors are the same as in other tribal cultures: the painting indicated age and status, as the young men between 17 and 30 were the most self-adorned and certain colors belonged to specific age-grades, and the most extravagant painting was connected to a time of dancing, celebration, ceremonial fighting and enhancing your attractiveness to the opposite sex. In their isolated cultural group, however, the Southeast Nuba went further. It became a personal art, as men would paint themselves daily, even when there was no ceremonial context for the painting.

The most insightful and rigourous study of bodypainting (tribal or otherwise) that I've read is *Nuba Personal Art* (1972) by James C. Faris. Through detailed visual analysis of their bodypaintings and interviews with the Southeast Nuba over three field sessions among them from 1966-1969, Faris decodes the visual language and, even more valuably for a working body artist, explains the methodology and principles that led to such stunning art. He offers charts that break down the visual grammar in algorithmic form using a structural analysis "derived from generative linguistics [which] regard the corpus of design forms as iconic grammar." Charts such as the basic symmetrical tribal face patterns which I re-created on a face in Chapter 1.

He offers insights through photographed faces as examples, such as the subjective difference to the viewer between two lines that come down from the eye and stop midway on the cheek, versus two lines which continue past the cheek and the ear to join the hair (the first seems to represent something, maybe the legs of an animal, while the second seems more like a pure design element because we don't see the end of the lines).

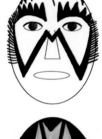

"Whatever the source of the designs used on the body, the critical factor is that the body must be emphasised, complemented, enhanced. No design or artistic treatment must detract from the presentation of the physical form itself—the chief reason, after all, for the personal art rests in the proper cultural exposure and celebration of the healthy body."

— *James C. Faris*

He describes the principles they follow to achieve what, to me, are their most amazing successes: the wildly asymmetrical face and body designs that are beautifully balanced. Before finding his book I tried to parse my own rules for balancing such designs by copying them and attempting my own on Congo theme days at the zoo—a gloriously frustrating endeavor. (Interestingly, the most open and asymmetrical of their design forms is termed *"kobera,"* which is also their generic term for "butterflies." Think of that the next time you are painting your 50th butterfly at a gig—and let yourself go asymmetrical and wild.)

He writes about their selection and use of animal imagery and how it is chosen not to give the wearer some totemic connection to the animal represented, but entirely for its value as a visual design and how well suited it is to the forms of a human body. The ostrich shape, as seen in the photo above, is painted over an eye not to give the wearer the speed of the ostrich but because the shape fits so well over the eye socket with the neck and head as a linear design running up the forehead and the two legs represented as diagonal lines, being an ideal shape to set against the curves of the cheek bone. It is a design that would be chosen by an artist with nice eyes, to draw attention to them.

This is the quality that sets the Southeast Nuba apart from other traditional body arts: the aesthetic value of the design and, especially, its ability to enhance the human form it is painted on are paramount to any meaning or ceremonial content in the design. Their goal is to celebrate the beauty of the human body by turning themselves into works of art.

There is no explanation for how this unique personal art first developed among these three villages, though their isolation was certainly a factor in its survival into the twentieth century. It seems to me that at some point in time aesthetics became as important as ritual and then everyone wanted to get attention as the best artist with the best looking body. Although Faris found no outside historical influences that led to this explosion of creativity, he does confirm something I have often thought about in viewing tribal body art: without mirrors, people painted each other and no one knew what they looked

like. He determined that after 1900, the Southeast Nuba were able to acquire mirrors from traders and the young men went from painting each other to painting themselves.

In the photographs of the Southest Nuba, every face design is different. The sketches on this page are from photos by Faris from 1966 to 1969. The sketches on the opposite page are from photos by Riefenstahl from 1974.

Face by Lorraine.

I wonder if that's when aesthetics and the desire to show off took over.

Even though it is practiced as an aesthetic act, their body decoration does satisfy the function that scholars describe as the fundamental reason behind all body art. As stated by Faris, without dependence on symbolic content, "the most meaningful element is the medium on which it is commonly produced—the human body. This culturally proper exposure can be, perhaps, as Lévi-Strauss has suggested, the essential expression of culturological man as opposed to the biological individual." It is our art that makes us human.

Having seen a few photos of Nuba body art in various books, I was first able to track down a copy of the book that most of them came from: *People of Kau* by Leni Riefenstahl. Whereas Faris's book is an anthropological study with photographs, hers is a real celebration of their art through photography. In 1974 she spent three months with the Southeast Nuba and recorded both their self-adornment and their ceremonies.

Leni Riefenstahl is famous (or notorious) for her documentary film *Triumph of the Will* (1934). In her dedication to *People of Kau* she writes of her desire to "record an ancient culture soon to be extinguished by the march of civilization" in much the same sentiment as artist George Catlin a hundred years earlier spoke of his portraits of the Plains Indians. The book is indeed a fascinating look into a unique culture. Too fascinating to be ignored, and thereby hangs a familiar

and bittersweet tale. Her photographs were so sensational that, according to the documentary *Worlds Apart: The Southeast Nuba* (1982, directed by Chris Curling), they helped accelerate the dissolution of this traditional culture as the villages became tourist destinations. Much of the tribal body art we see in the world today is done primarily for tourism. Young Kau men would no longer go into the fields to work during harvest season and instead would wait for the tourists to come and pay them to paint themselves for photographs.

Accompanying the preface to *Body Decoration* are two photographs. One is of a Nuba man in 1975 with a white and red asymmetrical face pattern, his naked body glistening with oil. The second photograph is of the same individual two years later fully clothed in European dress, wearing a baseball cap.

This is a vanished art, as the negative effects of exposure to tourists and the modern culture of money was compounded by the strife and civil wars that have plagued Sudan for decades. In a recent *National Geographic* magazine, I read that the Sudanese government is quite intolerant of traditional nakedness and body arts, and it is actively working to end the tribal culture of the various people of the Nuba mountains. The article reported that a primary weapon they are using to this end is satellite TVs, placed in community centers to lure the younger members of the tribes into a fascination with the modern world.

Twice a day, each Congo Summer weekend, we'd hear the infectious
drumming as the Harambee Dance Company approached, bringing
crowds of people to our facepainting tent. Thank you to the
Wildlife Conservation Society for the wonderful opportunity
to paint faces at their world-famous Bronx Zoo.
We can not imagine a better environment for adventurous
facepainting, with 25,000 excited people visiting there
each weekend day in the summertime.
People from all over the world.

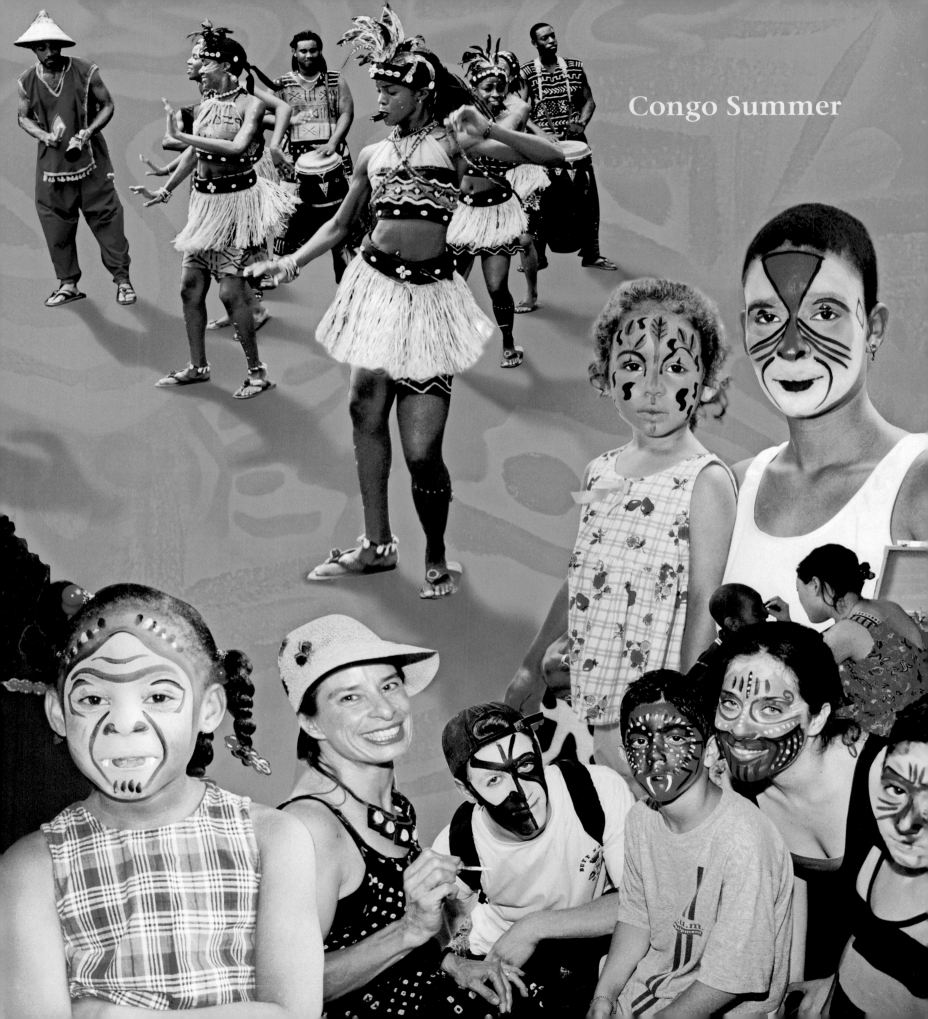

Congo Summer

*The Saint Francis Day Fair
at the Cathedral of
St. John the Divine, NYC*

5 Event Facepainting
creating modern masks

When you facepaint at an event, what do you do? I make art. I create it on people's faces. In my interaction with the person I paint, I transform them. By transforming individuals, I transform the event. That's my story and I'm sticking to it.

Lizi, Niru and Maria were with me painting at the 2005 St. Francis Day Fair. Some of the faces in this chapter were painted by them.

Facepainting is an ideal art form. The workplace environments are festive, the work smiles back at you and people pay you to do it. To the envy of your canvas-painting friends, you'll have 50 to 100 finished works of art at the end of a gig—and you always get to exhibit your work in public. Anyone who says the art is too ephemeral should check their fridge to see if there's a photo on it of someone's painted face.

To get to the faces I paint at events today, there was a progression that began with the usual clown faces and princesses, cheek and hand art, cartoons and superheroes. Early on I might have painted a Chinese Opera mask on an adventurous adult, but mostly I strived to do what people expected.

As I worked more, my goals changed and that changed what I wanted to paint. Working as an artist gets you to feel like an artist, or vice versa, so I became intent on making an art of my facepainting.

From the "Anthropometry" body prints by Yves Klein in the 1960s to the incredible work being done at the World Bodypainting Festival and other such events today, it is evident that an artist can do some serious painting on a human body. In the regular career of a face and body painter, however, the opportunities to spend hours creating fine art on a model are rare. Most of us spend our time painting people at parties and events. My aim was to find a way to work seriously as an artist on *all* my gigs, and that required a different approach.

The detail, shading and fine linework you'll put on a model for photography is impractical at a kid's birthday party or when you have a line of people waiting at an event. So how do you make art on someone's face quickly enough for the entertainment business?

Naoko and I were painting at a high profile benefit recently, and even though the first person I painted that night was a TV star, we had a line of waiting people so we were painting quickly. After watching us for a while, a man in a very nice suit leaned over my shoulder and quietly said to me, "You have taken a craft and elevated it to an art." He wasn't commenting on the brushwork or the quality of the blends (although those are some of the technical concerns we facepainters think about). He was responding to the designs we were painting. Each face was different. Each design used the face in a different way. There were masks, scenes and faces from other cultures. Although each was just a quickly painted face, collectively, they became art.

The Animal Fest

The photos in this chapter are from my favorite annual event. I first painted a face at the St. Francis Day Fair at the Cathedral of St. John the Divine in 1985, invited by a facepainter named Teddy Goldman. You can find the photo of me as a leopard that year in the next chapter. It's always held on the first Sunday of October. If you are ever in Manhattan on that day, I invite you to come see the blessing of the animals—a procession into the Cathedral, which some years has even included an elephant—and then stay to have your face painted. The Cathedral is a center for the arts as well as the spirit, and this fair draws a wonderfully eclectic crowd that really lets us be creative. In 2005 I painted one man who has written books about the Northwest Coast Indians whose masks I so admire, and swapped stories with another who knew the locations and political status of the various African tribes whose body art I study. Meeting such people reminds me of how little I know.

With twenty years of facepainting at this event, there were a lot of photographs to choose from. We decided to try to show what I do at one real event, using some of the same faces you'll find in the other chapters, so most of the photos in this chapter were taken by Lorraine at the 2005 fair (except as indicated). The theme, of course, was animals, and people were invited to tell us their favorite or to be surprised. After a couple of hours of facepainting, I gathered an audience for some informal "Transformation! Show" storytelling.

It was a beautiful day for pictures, blessed from the start when the mate of Pale Male, Manhattan's famous Red Tail Hawk, landed on a tree branch above to eat what she'd caught for breakfast.

When you take the work you do seriously, you want to do something special with it. At times it has seemed like an epic struggle to get people to accept my desire to put works of art on their faces, but it has gotten me to a place where I am paid by clients to do what I want to do, surrounded and supported by a company of artists, and confidant that when we work we are making art.

The second half of this book will explore how my colleagues and I have developed a creative, mask-conscious approach within the requirements of entertainment facepainting—and how we have used our willingness to experiment to develop a wider range of face ideas, specifically for some of the basic animals we all paint. First, though, I want to describe the *Transformation! Facepainting* approach to events.

In the mid-80s, I would be hired for large corporate picnics around New York along with other facepainters who mostly did cheek art. More people would get on my line than theirs because I was doing cat faces and such. There was a time when event producers thought anyone could facepaint, and when I heard one facepainter at a Pepsico picnic tell a child that she'd have to go to me because he didn't know how to paint a heart, I decided I needed help. The next time they called, I said I could bring a team of artists that painted like me and thus *Transformation! Facepainting* was born.

We worked to establish ourselves within the New York area as a facepainting company for corporate and public events, painting full faces quickly in bold designs that set us apart. Although we've lost some work along the way with clients who preferred a more familiar approach, by establishing a specific identity we achieved the business function of separating ourselves from the competition. We have discovered (or generated) a market for what we want to do.

I believe that you make a place for your self by doing what you do best, for you can't be all things to all people. There was a period when I spent a lot of time explaining to potential clients that the facepainting we did was different. Now, most of our jobs come from people who have seen us work and want what we offer, and we stay busy.

Maximum Impact: BE BOLD!

Facepainting is by nature a performance art because you do it with the public watching. That means it should be exciting to watch. There's the extra twist that your canvas has a life of its own, so you also want to make it fun to get painted and to wear the painted face. In most situations you are doing this as a hired entertainer and that has its own requirements.

Most facepainters begin with the goal of pleasing the person they paint. I started facepainting in a very

1999

public location as a member of a theater company and so began with what I view as the advantage of also being aware of the effect of my faces on the watching crowd. Over time, that gave me the impetus to offer event producers an approach to facepainting designed to enhance their whole event.

At most events we only do full-face designs to have the maximum visual impact. If facepainters can stay busy doing beautiful full faces that wow the crowd, they should skip the hands and small designs that are mostly for the delight of the wearer.

Because most people don't know what a good facepainter is capable of, they ask to get something they've seen before (kids especially), so part of an artist's job is to guide the process to where you can show them what you can really do. It may seem easier to give each person exactly what they ask for, but every painted hand means one less exciting face. As you can't paint everyone at a large event anyway, you might as well paint those people that will let you do your best work. At both our free public events and our fee-per-face concession we feel we have more success when we go with our strength and paint full faces that stand out in the crowd (and attract more people to get painted).

Paint a face not just for the person wearing it but also for the crowd watching—for the people who will see that face walking around the event or sitting with three other painted faces at the snack bar.

At a house party it's your responsibility to be spectacular—to give the client their money's worth. Kids might be satisfied by getting their hands painted, but how much richer is the experience when you paint faces instead, and all the kids interact as the creatures they've become?

We like to work large and bold when hired to bodypaint for private parties and evening events as well. Unlike alternatives like henna and temporary tattoos, bodypaintings are so temporary that there's little point in being too subtle to be easily noticed. Paint the guests so that they decorate the party.

Show off whenever you paint. That means really using your canvas (the face): painting large, being very creative and taking a certain amount of control over what you paint. Paint a face exciting enough to surprise the wearer. Paint the face not just for the person wearing it but also for the crowd watching, and also for the people who will see that face walking around the event or sitting with three other painted faces at the snack bar. The face should catch your eye from a distance. The elements of the face should still be clear from across the square. Each face on those four people sitting there should make a distinct impression. It should make you look and wonder. Especially, it should make you wonder if you can get painted too.

Paint *FAST*

In my stage presentations, I'm happy to paint one face with an audience of 300 watching. With a team of artists at an event, we want to paint all 300 of those faces—or as many as we can.

When we're really cooking, the actual painting time is a couple of minutes per face, so an artist will paint from 20 to 30 people in an hour. That's a lot of faces. With multiple artists over multiple hours the faces add up. Each face adds to the look of the event. With enough painted people a visual atmosphere is created.

We pay a lot of attention to logistics, to leave the artist free to concentrate on the face before them. For a team at an event, we organize just one line, preferably with staff to manage it. We use signs to let people waiting know what to expect—it is very important to let people know your "rules" *before* they've been waiting on line (like "full faces only" for our public events).

2002

2002

1994

Show off whenever you facepaint. That means really using your canvas (the face): painting large, being very creative and taking a certain amount of control over what you paint.

Most important for the crowd's comfort and to help speed things along, we maintain contact with them. We set up with at least one artist right near the line so people can see the face being painted and hear the interaction with the artist, which prepares them for their turn. Letting people watch as they wait is entertaining.

For public events in New York, the lines get very long. Painting fast is a necessity. It also fits my aesthetics for a painted face. I like faces that are simple and clear—faces that look good from a distance. For the quickest faces we take a very graphic approach which will be described via a tiger face in the next chapter. I don't believe we hurry anything in order to paint quickly at an event. Rather, we have a style and a technique that lets us work fast.

Paint *Everyone*

In my more radically artistic moments, I see what we do as a kind of guerrilla theater in which we turn the audience into the show. We want to paint everyone. We encourage the adults and teens to get painted along with the kids. I especially like to see whole families painted at our public events. It adds so much. The kids are thrilled to see their parents getting involved. To

see a painted adult walking around has more impact than a painted child. It is more surprising. It adds a legitimacy to our claim that we take our facepainting seriously—seriously enough for an adult to wear it. The inclusion of mask and cultural images has helped us to become attractive beyond the kid's market. Some clients tell us that they bring us to an event to get the teens involved, for a tribal design or a Kabuki mask is cooler than the latest superhero. We also get 20-somethings and adults without kids to sit down and get painted.

Adults are more fun to paint. They have big, beautiful faces with developed character that can inspire greater creativity. They are usually more willing to let you take risks, and have less expectations than a child has for what a certain face is supposed to look like. They give you an opportunity to show off.

We tell clients in advance that we are there to paint the big people as well as the little ones. The only age restriction we have is that we don't paint babies or toddlers, for we don't feel that facepainting is appropriate for the very young. At public events we clearly post "For adults and children age 3 and up."

Be Original

We like to be creative, not just in our over-all approach, but on every face we paint. If I get 20 people asking for a tiger face during a facepainting session, I want each of those 20 to look different. There would be a mix of naturalistic and mask-like faces: tigers with teeth and without, whole tigers leaping across the face, tiger eyes in a graphic stripe design, tigers in the style of Kathakali theater or Maori tattoo, helmet masks, and all the variations of painting elements like color and linework. Just changing the size and shape of the tiger's eyes can make two faces very different.

The best way to get the public to let you be creative on their faces is to be *very creative*.

People may sit down expecting to get the same face they've seen on someone else, but if every face they've seen is different their expectations expand. Our displays and presentation are designed to get people excited about being part of an artistic process (for example, we do not use photo menu boards which define how certain faces should look). We'll use our more familiar face designs on the youngest kids, but the older ones and the adults, especially, often enjoy getting something unique. It makes them feel special.

The best way to get the public to let you be creative on their faces is to be VERY creative.

We also "sell" a person on their face while we are painting them. Tell them why their tiger face is different than the last one: how you chose colors that match their eyes, or gave them big teeth to make their tiger dangerous, etc. Get them excited to look into the mirror at the end.

This approach makes facepainting as fun for the people watching as for the people who get painted—people want to see what you'll do next. It is a way of showing you are an artist and not just a craftsman. It elevates the response of the crowd and gets the adults to sit down and get painted.

It is our company policy to make every face at an event different. It's the mantra I use to constantly push myself into new directions for faces. To develop as an artist painting faces has not just meant perfecting the execution of my designs or of those inspired by others. It has meant being willing to try new ideas—to take risks on other people's faces. Risks mean failures, of course, so I am grateful to be a facepainter and not a tattooist. My failures wash off.

Over time you develop a repertoire that allows you to paint those 20 different tigers and which gives you the confidence to try a new idea for #21. Through creative experimentation, the repertoire you develop is not a set of specific repeatable designs but rather a set of visual tools—approaches to creating a face that can apply to any subject. Those 20 tiger concepts will help you do 20 different butterflies or Spidermans, too.

You need to work to build your personal repertoire by paying attention to the successful faces you paint: take photos, make sketches. A later chapter follows the process I used to develop a new set of ideas for cat faces.

Speaking of everyone's favorite arachnid super-hero, I gave up painting the latest fad during the summer of the Teenage Ninja Mutant Turtles. I liked the turtles and the rather hip comic books that started it all. The summer their movie came out, however, every little kid wanted to be one. The day I painted 50 in a row at a company picnic I decided, "enough." Not only did the repetition take the fun out of facepainting, it didn't let me show off what I could do. I needed to get away from painting only what people expected.

That has become part of our company approach: we do not paint any cartoons, characters or sports logos unless it's for the companies that promote them. (We were very happy to bring our approach to painting Horton and other Dr. Seuss characters, for example, for his anniversary celebration hosted by the Children's Museum of Manhattan). There is also a very practical reason for avoiding pop culture images: it is easy to blow it. A sports logo that's even a little off looks bad. Painting a superhero brings a set of expectations you have to satisfy, and when you do, all you have achieved is copying someone else's art. Also, I no longer feel the need to put my art in the service of some corporation's blockbuster movie.

In place of superheroes we have gravitated towards animal designs. Almost any kid has a favorite animal they might want to become. Animals became part of our company identity as we got consistent clients like the Bronx Zoo and the annual St. Francis Day Fair at the Cathedral of St. John the Divine. As we realized that animal faces didn't always need to be realistic we appreciated them even more as vehicles for mask exploration and general creativity. Today our usual offerings at an event include 1) animal and nature images in all sorts of realistic, mask-like or scenic designs; 2) other concepts that allow for creativity like monsters, princesses, and clowns; and 3) what I think of as the classics: mask and makeup designs from world cultures.

Make Your Facepainting into a Show

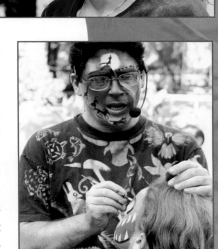

The ultimate freedom to be creative comes when you make your facepainting into a show—because everyone wants to be part of a show. We take a theatrical approach to the presentation of our facepainting at large events. We set up so that both the people waiting and an interested crowd can watch us work. We play music to create an atmosphere—which for us means world music, ethnographic recordings and tribal drumming. We wear costuming that relates to the faces we paint to show we have a vision about what we do. Whenever possible we paint each face for free, with the event producer or a sponsor paying our fee—so that the only decision people have to make is whether they want to get painted, not how much it will cost.

For some events I wear a microphone to explain what we're doing or to tell the story behind the face I'm painting. I'll do a series of mask-inspired designs or a set of variations on one face idea to show that we are taking this very creative approach, so they need to give us artistic freedom. For events with unusual themes, I'll tell them they will be getting unusual faces—but not to worry, it washes off. When I do my full stage show beside a team of artists we don't even ask people what they want to be: I tell them that everyone gets a surprise today because we want to show them all the different ways we have to paint a face.

The quality and creativity of the faces is the ultimate vehicle for success, so the primary ingredient of performing as a facepainter is showing off on the faces you paint. And you can show off in any situation.

As artists develop within our company, I ask them to find their own set of "classics": twelve spectacular faces they paint that will make someone go, "wow." The classics are a way to draw attention at an event. If you already have a crowd's attention, they are a way to elevate their appreciation for what you do.

These are also great faces for the birthday boy, or for the host of the party.

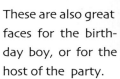

If you want to be seen as an artist painting faces, you have to demonstrate that you have the chops. When the first adult sits down after a line of kids, give them a face that stands out. When a bald guy wants to become a tiger, spend the extra minutes to give him a full-head crowd-stopper. Show off.

I think we have a primary responsibility as artists and entertainers to show people what our art is capable of, in all settings.

There are so many talented facepainters working around the country today, I am surprised that the public still does not expect much when they sit down to get their faces painted. Until you show them what's possible, most people will keep asking for the same things they've had painted before.

Although facepainting can be presented as a commodity intent on giving each individual something for their own enjoyment, our best clients understand that we are there for the general entertainment of the entire event. We present facepainting as an interactive performance art offering the ultimate in audience participation as everyone we paint is transformed into a work of art.

To present our facepainting as an art, we take control of the process in a way that allows us to bring people past their expectations and which, therefore, lifts the value of the experience for those getting painted. Anytime you can get the public to go beyond their expectations (especially with crazy themes like "Rain Forest Faces" or "everyone gets a surprise," or even if it's just by not painting superheroes or the current fad) you are getting them to join you in the adventure. They make a choice to become part of the show.

With this creative approach, each individual gets his or her own special identity as we paint them. Each face is different, so each face draws interest from those watching. Their experience of being painted is enriched by the response of the people to their face throughout the event. Even those who don't get painted vicariously experience the transformation as an event fills with interesting faces. In the process, we get to paint some very cool faces that make our clients happy and that keep it all exciting for us as well.

We facepainters can do more than decorate people when we paint them. By making the process of being painted exciting and exotic, striving for a creativity and quality that makes each face amazing—by making each person feel special as they walk away with a unique face—we can give them a subjective experience of being transformed into a supernatural new identity. By painting as artists, we can achieve in a modern context the profound potential of this ancient art.

The St. Francis Day Fair is full of good memories, and also has been a very lucky event for us. One year a face I painted was photographed by Amy Arbus for the Village Voice, and she later photographed the "Neon Tiger" face that I've used on postcards for years.

In 1999, Bruce Weber saw me there and a few weeks later I was in a swamp in Florida painting 18 models for an Abercrombie & Fitch catalog he was shooting. Here are a couple of my snapshots from that session.

We used this type of graphic representation of a tiger in 1997 on a promotional postcard. We got such a good response that I thought it could become a logo image for our company. At Big Cats Weekend in 1999 I painted several versions of this concept on people and took photographs of them all. This photo became our logo: "The Eyes."

6 The Essence of a Tiger

This is a face I call "The Eyes." It is simple, clear, effective and very quick to paint—an exemplar of our company style. It's a painted mask designed to *signify* a tiger. Like a traditional mask, it is neither a decoration of the face nor a realistic portrait of the tiger. It is the essence of the tiger.

What makes a tiger a tiger?

I believe it's more important to paint the idea of an animal than what an animal really looks like. This is a very functional approach for a facepainter. Thanks to anthropologist Claude Leví-Strauss, we have the rationale behind it that to represent an animal, a mask must have the distinguishing feature(s) that signify that it is not representing any other animal (my standard example: a snake gets fangs and a forked tongue) —after satisfying that requirement, the mask maker can be creative. For me, the essence of the cat is the eyes. When you add stripes to the eyes, the cat becomes a tiger.

These are not the eyes of a real tiger. People think of tigers, lions, etc. as "big cats" and we so admire the mysterious slit eyes of our house cats. The big cats like tigers actually have round pupils, but painting them that way seems to jar our mental image of a cat. Part of painting the "idea of an animal" is incorporating how people *think* it looks (thus a snake gets fangs even though you rarely see the fangs of a live snake), and so most of my big cat faces get the same iconic slit eyes that represent all cats.

These are not the stripes of a real tiger because you should never let reality stand in the way of a good design. Whereas a real tiger's stripes curve gently around the face, these stripes are stronger. They radiate out from between the eyes as do the stripes in the classic samurai pattern from Japanese Kabuki on page 34. Just as the essential imagery of the tiger is "eyes plus stripes", the essential symbolic meaning of the tiger is "power." These radiating stripes in combination with these slit eyes graphically express a feeling of power. That is why I consider this a successful design.

Claude also warns that you need to avoid putting on a mask signifiers that will suggest it is something other than the animal you intend (so don't put fangs on a lizard face). This can get trickier. What makes a tiger not a tiger? Did you know that tigers have pink noses? I think that most people don't know that, and putting a pink nose on a tiger clashes with our mental image and the tiger's function as a symbol of power (and it clashes with the orange). So no pink noses.

The color orange helps suggest "tiger," but experience shows it is not essential. I like to stay within the range of colors of the real animal and work instead creating variation through design and placement on the face. Some of my facepainters are much more free with their animal colors and still, if it has cat eyes and stripes, people see it as a tiger.

 TRANSFORMATION FACEPAINTING

The Eyelid Trick

There is a difference between decorating a face and creating a mask. There is also a difference between placing a physical mask over the face and painting the mask onto the face. A facepainted mask will move and live. Transforming the features of a person's face moves your facepainting from the realm of decoration towards a painted mask. Using someone's eyelids for the eyes of a cat is more than a popular trick. It makes the wearer of the makeup an active participant in the transformation. As they open and close their eyes they bring the mask to life.

As I saw what could be achieved with facepainting, I knew that I didn't want to decorate people. I wanted to transform them—to turn them into something new. That is a primary function of theatrical makeup as I first learned it: to create a new character. I came to facepainting as part of a theater company that opened a concession at Adventureland Amusement Park in 1977 and our initial approach came out of the techniques of theatrical makeup. For the clown faces we began our concession with, we'd change the features of the face first (the nose, the mouth and the eyes) rather than depending on decorative elements like hearts and stars.

As I moved into painting animal faces, that primary focus remained and I worked to change the features of the human face into the features of the animal. The first time I painted eyes onto eyelids was in 1983 at Venice Beach, California.

Here's the photograph of that face, in the inset on the facing page. She had asked me to make her into a tiger like one drawn on a button I was wearing. While I was painting, she asked if I could give her "cat eyes," and while she sat there with her eyes closed, it seemed natural to paint the whole cat eye onto her eyelid. Eureka! I thought I had discovered gold. I thought I'd revolutionized facepainting! Of course, I hadn't. Who knows how many facepainters around the country were using the same trick. After thousands of years of mask traditions, one doesn't really invent anything in this art. In his classic makeup, the Monkey King of the Chinese Opera (Chapter 3) has worn eyes on his eyelids for at least a couple of hundred years. I'd first seen Chinese Opera faces in a magazine from 1980, so I had that image in my subconscious as I thought I was discovering the eyelid trick—though I wonder now why it took me three years to try such a wonderful idea. Comparing this photograph with the "eyes" variation behind it reminds me just what a long, strange trip it's been.

It still works. It still wows the crowd when you are painting in public. For years we were known around New York as the facepainters that do the eyes.

From using the two eyes as the eyes of the animal, it naturally follows to use one eye for an animal in profile, or leaping across the face. And so to use the mouth for an animal, especially an animal known for its teeth, like a shark. Much of the conceptual process I go through when designing a new animal face is how I can best transform the features of the human face into the features of the animal so that the mask is alive.

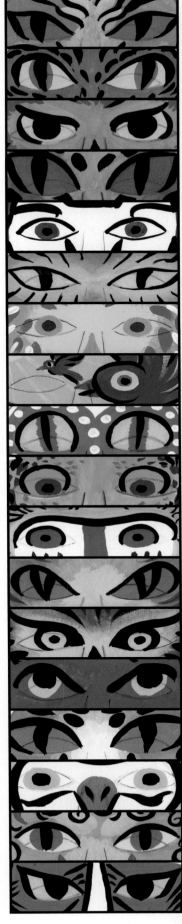

Another crowd pleaser is to give your big cat some big teeth. Here's a design we call the "helmet mask," the facepainted version of a mask concept with a wide variety of classical examples. It's based on masks worn over the whole head with the wearer's face visible through the open mouth of the animal—like a football helmet.

There are some events at which your facepainting has to become a show even if you are not on stage. It may be a private party with fewer guests than expected or a corporate event where you're not as busy as you'd like to be. In those cases, every face you paint counts and you prove you are worth the big bucks by showing off on those few faces.

Develop some sensational designs that can be show stoppers. Make them big and bright so they can't be missed at an event. Have a few ready for those powerful looking guys in suits—I tell my facepainters they get extra points for painting those guys. If you get a willing bald guy to sit down, take advantage of the extra canvas.

Lorraine took some extra time to paint this man in the photo at left who was one of the organizers at a company picnic. Doing a fantastic job on the people in charge is another way to earn points at an event.

I painted this man on the right at the start of a special event for government officials and their families. We were doing their kids, but I didn't think we'd be getting a lot of the adults to sit down. So I wanted to make this one count. At the end of the evening he returned to thank me. So many people had stopped to look at him and take photographs that he had felt like the life of the party.

The Helmet Mask

New York kids love to visit the collection of knights in shining armor at the Metropolitan Museum of Art. You can find a golden helmet there in the shape of a roaring lion that was worn by an Italian knight in 1460.

It is a warrior's mask meant to evoke the idealized power of the mythical hero Herakles (Hercules). In the first of his twelve labors, Herakles slew the Nemean Lion and from then on wore its head and skin in a classic example of the general totemic use of animal symbols in many cultures: by wearing the token of powerful animals you acquire their power. It's a great way to frighten off your enemy: "don't mess with me, I'm the one who killed him." On coins from ancient Greece, Alexander the Great is also depicted wearing a lion-headed helmet.

We use this helmet mask design concept for dinosaurs, crocodiles, sharks—all the big cats like this jaguar on the right— and it makes a nice baboon variation as shown below. It works great for anything with big teeth.

Today, the masks of Mexico keep alive a similar tradition of the Mayan, Aztec and Toltec cultures, as seen in their sculptures of warriors wearing helmet masks with jaguar, eagle, serpent or coyote imagery. In my reproduction of a Mayan ruler from the painted walls at Bonompak, Mexico, he wears a

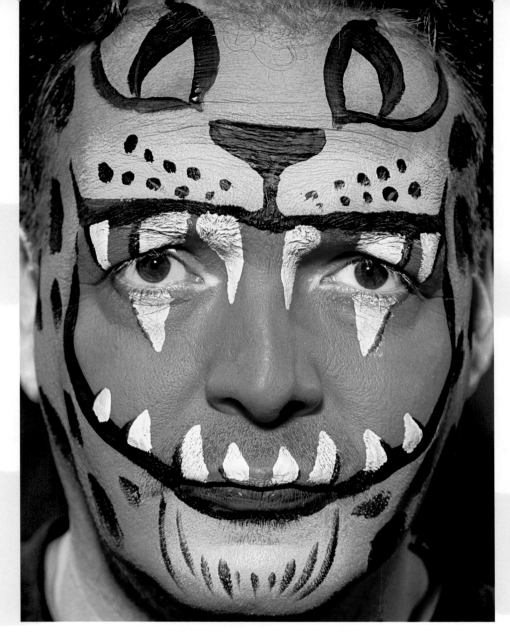

jaguar mask on his head and an additional mask indicated by the faint line in front of his face. The second example is a modern wooden mask from Chiapas in which the dancer's face appears through the gap where the tongue is.

The fantastic examples of Aztec Eagle Warrior sculptures take the transformation a step further as the human warrior's face is fully enclosed within the beak of a giant eagle head —as if the human is a spirit inhabiting an idealized eagle form. Think about that while you paint your next face.

WHAT IF... Painting the same animal so often offers a great opportunity for the "what if" game. What if a tiger were painted as a Chinese Opera face, or an African mask, or by Picasso? These faces all have the same basic cat features, each handled with a different stylistic approach. One of the things we've seen through pushing ourselves towards creative variety is that there are so many ways to successfully paint a face. The four at the bottom all feature teeth in mouths with different shapes and placement on the face, and they all work.

TRY IT!

A Tiger As Quick As a Cheetah

For events where you can't see the end of the line of people waiting for you, here's my simplest tiger face. Just two sponge colors and black. It doesn't take more than 90 seconds to comfortably paint this face, as in this example painted at an event in 2005.

ORANGE Start with a sponge and orange makeup for the base color. Leave the skin exposed on the eyelids and around the mouth where you put in the yellow.

YELLOW I use a large, round sponge to apply my base makeup. By squeezing the working area of the sponge between my thumb and fingers I can control the shape it makes to put the yellow almond shape of a cat's eye onto the eyelids. By adjusting the size and shape of the eyes you can change the demeanor of the cat: large eyes are cute and kittenish, while narrower eyes can be made sinister. Yellow also goes over and beneath the lips for the whisker areas. When I am working quickly I don't take a lot of time to blend my colors together, but I can make variations in tone by stippling the yellow over the orange. My sponges have an open texture so if I gently touch them to a face I can quickly stipple on some color to create highlights and a furry texture.

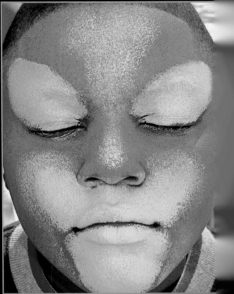

BLACK Finally, the black line work. The essential methodology of my fast event faces is strong black line work over brightly colored bases. I'll use a black liquid makeup loaded onto a #8 round brush when working at my quickest. Eyes first, so they can set a bit while I finish the rest. Iconic cat eyes, with a vertical line for the pupil, also have the advantage that they don't smear if wet when you open your eyes (like a rounded pupil does). A tiger's face and nose are longer than ours, so you need to create an illusion to help change the shape of the human face to be more tiger-like. For the nose: paint an upside down black triangle extending below the human nose to make it look longer. Beside the nose, draw a line down from the corner of each eye to the nose you made and shade that line out a bit under the eye with the edge of your brush to make the human nose seem wider. Add the distinctive line cats have from the nose to the lips. Then paint just the bottom lip black (not the top lip at all) to help complete a visual illusion that makes the whole whisker area jut forward. Support this illusion with the curve of the lines extending out from the sides of the bottom lip, and with "fur" lines on the chin framing the yellow patch. For whiskers I use dots (because I think they read better than little lines which can look like stripes in the wrong place). Add dynamic black stripes and the tiger is done.

This is by no means a subtle tiger face, but the lack of fine details does not mean there is a lack of artistry. It's just designed to be quick, strong and to look great from across the room.

So Many Big Cats

In one of my favorite photographs, a group that five of us had painted on a Big Cats Weekend at the Bronx Zoo gathers around Roberta to watch her finish the final face. For twelve years, our summers at the zoo included this three-day special event at which we only painted lions, tigers, jaguars, cheetahs, etc. It was a healthy challenge to approach such limited subject matter with our desire to make every face different. It forced our artists to experiment with colors, line work and finding additional inspiration via world masks and such (the "what if" approach). Experimentation leads to discovery.

More people ask us to turn them into cats than any other animal, especially the big cats like tigers. When you are painting your 20th tiger face in a row and you're dying to try your new warthog design it can be frustrating (Lorraine's trick is to make the tigers increasingly tribal or abstract until people start asking for something else), but it is also comforting to know there's one face just about everybody is happy to get.

We painted groups of school kids for the opening ceremonies of the Tiger Mountain Exhibit in 2003. The several "tigers only" weekends that followed pushed me even further to find a new concept for my cats that I describe in Chapter 10. Like Conan the Barbarian said, "What doesn't kill you, makes you stronger."

1988

On behalf of all facepainters,
I want to thank cats everywhere.
Not only is their dramatic
appearance inspiring to paint,
they also inspire people to
get painted.

1991 at Mardi Gras

1985 at Unique, NYC

1989 "Neon Tiger" – photograph by Amy Arbus

1999

2005

1999

1989

1999

1995

1985 – My First St. Francis Day Fair

85

Whereas the essential tiger eyes became the logo for our facepainting, the Monarch Butterfly has always been the icon for our performing arts company. Pictured here is my wife Lorraine having become a butterfly in a scene for the first show we created together. The scene was derived from the ancient Taoist writings of Chuang Tsu, who dreamed of being a butterfly and woke to ask, "did I dream I was the butterfly, or did the butterfly dream it was me?" For years I had the final line of that passage on my makeup kit: "...this is a case of transformation."

7 Butterflies & Beautiful Faces

How fitting that butterflies are one of the most requested faces. The butterfly is the symbol for miraculous transformation—of any kind. Who would look at a caterpillar and think it could become a butterfly? They also represent the beauty of Nature in an idealized form.

Ah, butterflies. My gardens include their favorite flowers so I can watch them flying around in the summer sun. The stories and poems they inspire fill our shows, including the incredible true story of the Monarch Butterfly's annual migration from Mexico to Canada and back—a nature tale emblematic of both the power and fragility in these beautiful creatures. Here's the metamorphosis cycle of a Monarch that stopped in my garden to share its miracle, from caterpillar through chrysalis to butterfly, and the design it inspired as painted on the beautiful face of my daughter, Chloe.

A Butterfly Breakdown

The beautiful butterfly possesses such an archetypal image that its pictorial representation comes with some limitations. Something like a tiger offers more elements: you can add teeth or claws to the iconic eyes and stripes; give the face a range of expressions from cute to mean; or use images of the tiger leaping, etc. Butterflies are just "beautiful wings." In mask terms, their wings are their single significant element. You can not, for example, make someone's face the actual face of a butterfly because no one would recognize what they are without the wings.

The wings are distinctively triangular. Butterflies are two triangles touching at the point. Add a line in between and you have the graphic representation of a butterfly. It is a very effective design form.

The two triangles fit so naturally over the eyes that any other placement on the face seems awkward. So for a full face you usually put the two wings over the eyes like a mask. You can do one wing over one eye for a butterfly in profile and use the other side of the face for flowers and such. You can also take the scenic route and make a beautiful landscape with one or more smaller butterflies.

What the facepainter really gets to play with are the butterfly's decorative elements like wing patterns and bright colors. You can't change a butterfly's expression but you can give it style. You can go for realistic combinations or you can be wildly colorful and inventive. With some 17,00 o species of butterflies in the world, any choice you make will probably look like some beautiful something flying around out there.

One of the earliest butterfly face photos I have, from Halloween in LA, 1983

This is me from 1984 at Unique Clothing, NYC

Face by Dennis, 1999 photograph by Michael Mella

Face by Jennifer, 2005

July 1996 (Ngere-inspired)

September 1996 (African Textiles)

June 1997 (Chinese Opera)

July 1997 (Maori)

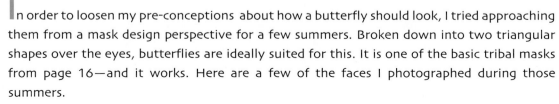

Chasing Butterflies...

The butterfly's dilemma: Is it possible for something to be too pretty?

For a facepainter, butterflies are their own eternal fad. Paint one beautiful butterfly at the start of an event and you may spend the rest of the day painting butterflies. So how do you have a facepainting adventure when you are painting butterflies?

In order to loosen my pre-conceptions about how a butterfly should look, I tried approaching them from a mask design perspective for a few summers. Broken down into two triangular shapes over the eyes, butterflies are ideally suited for this. It is one of the basic tribal masks from page 16—and it works. Here are a few of the faces I photographed during those summers.

In 1996 and '97, I took cultural styles and used them to "translate" a butterfly face, like the "what if" game from the previous chapter. I especially liked the Ngere-inspired design from July 1996 because it reminded me of seeing a butterfly in flight when it's all just moving colors with no distinct pattern. The Maori-esque spirals showed up in July 1997 and that became a model for some of the fancier butterflies I still paint, usually with more delicate black swirls on blended color wings. At a few events in 1998 I made no attempt to create a realistic butterfly and just played with the elements of color and decorative patterns within the mask form that the butterfly shape so naturally makes over the eyes. I'd start the face by choosing an element, like "dots," and see what I could do with it. Even an unsuccessful face such as the yellow one with the big spots can be a helpful step to a better design.

Some painters have rules for what they paint. I may have guidelines, but no rules. I'll try anything. A facepainter once told me that the wings have to fit between the middle of the forehead and the middle of the cheek, but I am flexible. I also do not require all my butterflies to be "pretty." In a day's work, my artists and I will do enough pretty butterflies that it's ok that some of the others are "amazing," "exciting" or even "interesting" instead.

And you don't have to be pretty to be beautiful.

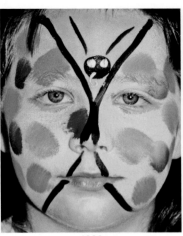

1998

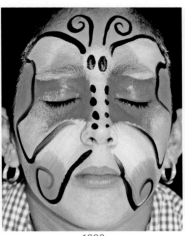

1998

1998

The Butterfly Girls

To select faces for this chapter I looked through my foto files and realized that although I certainly haven't stopped painting pretty butterflies on the many little girls we paint at events, I have mostly stopped taking pictures of those faces. Most of the snapshots I take lately are of the newer designs I am working on, the mask imagery I'm investigating or the more unusual things—the faces that surprise me. There were enough in the archives to help tell the story on the following pages. For some current examples, we got some of my daughter's friends together and had a very fun day painting them up and taking photographs of pretty butterflies on pretty girls.

The Butterfly Girls Go Around the World

Here they are with butterfly faces based on some of the cultural designs from the first half of the book. From left to right: Anya went to Japan for a Kabuki butterfly; Indira went to the Huli people on Papua New Guinea; Cassandra's design is inspired by the Southeast Nuba of Sudan; Helena's face is a re-imagined "shattered face" pattern from the Chinese Opera; and Chloe has become a butterfly goddess from the Kerala region of India.

A Butterfly Story That You Can Tell

The people say that there was a Creator of all things, who made the world of nature for the people to live in. One day late in the summer, Creator was sitting in the village watching the children play. The sky was so blue and the sun so bright. It was such a beautiful day that all the children were outside playing: running, jumping, laughing. Watching the children play, Creator became sad, for he had seen something that the children had not. He had seen that the leaves on the trees were starting to change color.

Do you know what it means when the leaves change color? That's right. Fall was coming. Soon the leaves would fall from the trees. Soon the summer days would be over and the nights would get long and cold. Soon all the beautiful summer flowers would wither and die. Creator was saddened, knowing what the passing of time would mean to the people. And he knew that the children would not be so happy during the long, grey winter. So he decided to make one more thing. Something to remind the children of that summer day.

He took his bag, and into it he put a little bit of all the colors of the summer day. He took some yellow from the sunshine and put that into his creation bag. He took some orange from a flower and put that into the creation bag.

Here's where you can help me with the story, for there are so many beautiful colors in the world of nature. Think of your favorite color, then think of something you might see on a summer's day that is that color.

Maybe he took some blue from the sky. Maybe he took red from a rose, or brown from the bark of a tree. Maybe he found green in the grass beneath their feet, or from the shell of a turtle, or the feathers of a bird. He took white from the smiles of the children playing and put that into the bag. There are so many places where you can find colors. Make a picture in your mind of something you might see in nature, when you're walking around outside on a summer's day, and take some of the color from that picture and put it into the bag.

When I learned this story I imagined there would be little pieces of color flying from everywhere to fill the creation bag, filling the bag so full that colors would be spilling out.

Then Creator gathered the children together and gave them his bag. He told them there was something nice inside, something for them. When they opened the bag, out flew butterflies. Hundreds and hundreds of butterflies. Dancing in the air around their heads. Making a sight so beautiful they would always remember it, even through a long and cold winter. And whenever they thought of the butterflies, they knew that summer, with all its beautiful colors,
would one day return.

The butterfly story was part of the first facepainting show I developed for family audiences. My initial inspiration was the balloon show of Allyn Gooen. We shared a stage at a physical comedy festival in which I did a solo clown act. He used twisted balloon costumes on audience volunteers to re-enact Godzilla attacking Tokyo. In between wiping tears of laughter from my eyes I thought, why not try it with facepainting?

To tell the butterfly story, I ask for a volunteer and say that what they will become is a surprise. They sit on a stool facing away from the audience as I paint, and I only turn them around to reveal the butterfly face at the end when the children in the story open the creation bag. The colors I use come from the audience. I'll start off with the yellow of the sun and orange from a flower and then get kids to raise their hands to suggest colors and tell me where they might see that color in nature. I add each color to the face as they suggest it. After I reveal the butterfly face (and the audience goes "oooh"), I show the volunteer his or her face in a mirror.

Facepainting a story works in other ways as well. You can illustrate the story step-by-step on a face, letting the audience watch. You can use several volunteers to be painted as the various animals or characters in a story as it progresses. You can paint audience volunteers and then have them act out whatever they've become. Or paint a face one way as you start the story and then change it as that character changes, which I do in my re-telling of a Chinese legend in which the heroine becomes a fish.

The audience gets to guess what birds I'm painting for the Owl and the Rooster folktale. I paint the owl facing me and reveal it only when the audience guesses. This very simple rooster I paint facing the audience, adding hints as I go: sunrise...rooftop...loud voice... fancy tail...it's a rooster!

Demonstrating and explaining a face like the Helmet Mask can also be a story.

Finding stories is almost as much fun as telling them. Folktale collections are the best source, especially those with simpler versions of the tales so that you get to add your own voice and embellishments. Try to get a few versions of a traditional tale so you can take the parts you like best and mix them up to make it your own. You can find a story first and design the faces to fit, or you can come up with a story to fit your best faces.

I was asked to come up with an inspirational folktale about personal sacrifice for an executive meeting at an oil company whose logo is the tiger. I couldn't find an appropriate story so I wrote one by explaining the source for each of the colors that I put on my basic tiger face. I didn't get the corporate gig, but I came away with the tale of *"The Tiger That Went To the House of the Sun."*

The open mouth shark face in Chapter 9 was destined for a story from the first time I painted it. It waited patiently for years before I found a Hawaiian tale I could adapt for it.

Faces also have their own intrinsic stories apart from any folktale. An audience may be just as interested in hearing about how you paint a face, where the inspiration came from, or any of the comic anecdotes we all gather in this funny business.

To develop my stories I tell them offstage as well, one-on-one to the kid I am painting at a party or event. It's a way to learn the essential story, what parts need to be clear and what parts you can either skip or embellish.

If you are taking your act onto the stage, remember that while the face you paint may provide the "wow," it's the story that matters most. Here's my best advice about the storytelling: listen to the audience, listen for their silence.

With regard to the facepainting, the simplified, graphic style I favor works for painting on stage. Fine details and subtle shadings are lost on a large audience. The face has to read from the back of the house.

You want to be able to maintain eye contact with the audience and you want to be able to concentrate on what you are saying. The faces can't be too complex. Nor do they need to be painted perfectly. A large audience is very forgiving, so don't sweat the details.

I am not a folklorist, I am a performer. I don't preserve stories, I bring them to new life. To present a traditional story to a modern audience requires alterations—as storytellers say, "never let the facts get in the way of the truth."

The butterfly story has changed a great deal in the telling since I found it in *American Indian Myths and Legends* (1984), which is part of a wonderful series of folktale collections from Pantheon Books. I didn't realize just how different it had be-

come until I sent my version of it to Janet, one of our facepainters, who happened to be doing a theater project among the tribe it belongs to. She replied that the winters aren't very cold in the Arizona desert where they live and that fall is the growing season, not summer. But I tell this tale to audiences in the Northeast and have changed it in the telling to fit our seasons.

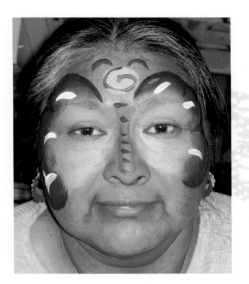

Even the name of the tribe has changed. The book identified the people who originated this tale as the Papago, but that is the name outsiders gave them. Their tribe officially changed their name to Tohono O'odham (Desert People) in 1986. Janet painted faces while she was there, including this beautiful Grandmother Butterfly.

For this show at a middle school I started by painting four cultural masks as the audience came in and used them to explain the origins and uses of facepainting. Then I told "The Tiger Who Went to the House of the Sun", followed by the classic folktale in which Spider Anansi meets the Sky God, illustrated on five faces in African mask styles. I ended with the story about the first time a man ever met a crocodile.

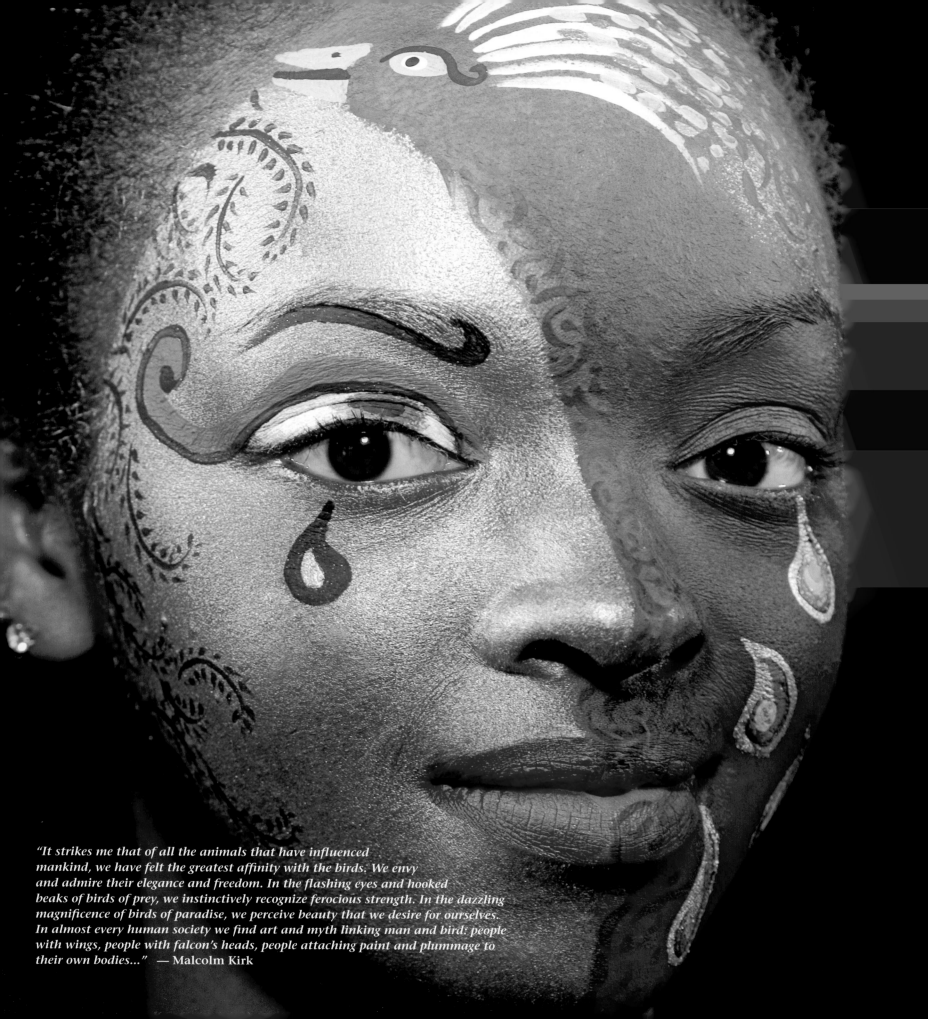

"It strikes me that of all the animals that have influenced mankind, we have felt the greatest affinity with the birds. We envy and admire their elegance and freedom. In the flashing eyes and hooked beaks of birds of prey, we instinctively recognize ferocious strength. In the dazzling magnificence of birds of paradise, we perceive beauty that we desire for ourselves. In almost every human society we find art and myth linking man and bird: people with wings, people with falcon's heads, people attaching paint and plummage to their own bodies..." — Malcolm Kirk

8 Free As a Bird

The Raven, bringing light to the world...
The Peacock, marrying the Sun Goddess...
The Phoenix, rising from the ashes...
Look, up in the sky! It's a bird!

In Mexican folklore, the hummingbird was here before the world was born, freshening the mouth of the Creator with drops of dew and feeding him with the nectar of flowers. Flying so high above us, dwelling as they do in the realm of the gods, it is no wonder that birds fill our myths. They are the symbols of our aspirations. We put bird's wings on our angels.

Can we understand what a bird soaring above meant to our ancestors? A hunter could be as deadly as a snake, as dangerous as a tiger. In the water he could swim like the fish. Running through the forest he might feel as swift as a deer. So many of the animal powers were within human ability. But only a bird could fly like that.

Whereas tigers are a symbol of power and butterflies a symbol for beauty and transformation, I see birds as a symbol of freedom. The freedom of flight, certainly, and a spiritual freedom as well. Freedom from the earthly realm. Free to move between this realm and the celestial one. A symbol for the spirit.

Once I sat on a hilltop in California and watched a hawk soaring high above me. It floated on the air currents, effortless. I watched as a smaller hawk, flapping its wings, rose up to join it. The smaller bird would soar alongside the larger for a few minutes before it spiraled back down. Then flap, flap, flap, it would climb again to the large hawk which continued to soar effortlessly.

I imagined I was watching a mother bird teaching its baby how to fly. That hawk made it look so easy. It hardly moved a wing. As if flying were a state of being. I wondered, if I watched long enough, would it teach me too?

Birds also inspire a freedom in their depiction on the human face. The swiftness of their flight, the softness of their feathers, invites a looseness to your imagery and brush strokes. Their freedom from the earth allows you to move them around the face. And so many types of creatures are described by that one word: bird. From the majestic eagle, to the graceful swan, to the exotic parrot, to the ridiculous chicken.

The hummingbird was also the messenger of the gods and could turn into a bolt of lightening to carry out their vengeance. In battle he would fly in the night over the camps of his enemies and kill their chief as he slept .

This is from a day when we were very busy at a large company's family picnic. I wanted to take advantage of this man's head, but I had to work quickly. So I used my biggest brushes to make this very BOLD eagle with no black linework at all.

You can put a bird on a person's face in quite a number of ways. Their appearance—and the difference in appearance of the many types of birds—lends itself to a great variety of approaches. Their wings are their most significant feature, but the ways of depicting a bird's wings are more flexible than a butterfly's. There are other features to work with as well: beak, eyes, tails, claws, feathers. Birds' eyes and beaks are distinctive enough that you can give someone a hawk's face, for example, without showing the wings at all, just as you might make a tiger face. Or, as you would with a butterfly, you could give them a birds' wing mask over both eyes.

A bird in flight is an iconic, recognizable form, so I use simplified images of small flying birds for both scenic faces (such as flock of birds silhouetted against a colorful sky) and as a graphic element in decorative face designs. Once you get the basic form of a bird down, you can use it for anything, from a pretty parakeet to a powerful eagle with simple adjustments of colors and details.

If the ability of a bird to fly is what makes it a symbol of freedom, then to express the essential meaning of a bird, you should show it in flight. My favorite approach is to paint a bird flying across the face, either in profile over one eye or with the bird's head on the forehead. It allows you to depict the full bird with all its significant features, including the beautiful wings. When I paint bird's wings I am inspired to keep my brushwork loose, ranging from dynamic lines expressing their movement and power to swirls and dashes of color for the softness of the feathers.

Using the eye for the eye of a bird in profile was an obvious step from learning to turn a person's two eyelids into cat eyes. It also leads into other profile images like the dragons in the next chapter. A bird over the eye is such a flexible image that you can bring any style into it. On the following page I trace my experimentation with different styles over the years by looking at some one-eye birds and their beautiful wings.

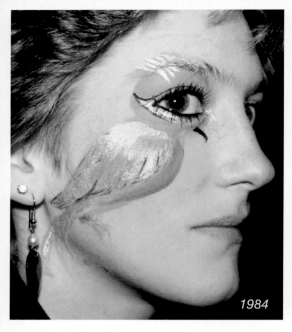

1984

1991

1997

2004

View of a Bird's Eye

This glittery bird from 1984 is more of an eye decoration than a mask image. I used stronger lines in the more realistic bluebird from a company picnic in 1991 as it became increasingly important to me to create images that transformed the face—and I remember getting a very positive reaction to this design. Going from one bird to a flock in a blue sky was one of the ways I began to use the face as a canvas to create scenes. This one from 1997 was painted on a beautiful party guest at the Cooper Hewitt Design Museum, the type of setting that encouraged me to think like an artist. The tropical bird from 1999 is looser, focusing more on color and design and less on realism. That led to a deliberately stylized approach that flattened the image and hid the human face. This graphic depiction of a bluebird against the sun was our company postcard in 2002. I continue to explore ways to use a bird to obscure the human face, like this toucan, or the two-winged pink parrot that shows I'm still working out where to place the lower wing to hide the nose. During the summer of 2004, I also fooled around with creating illusions by putting multiple animals on the face, illustrated by the three parrots here.

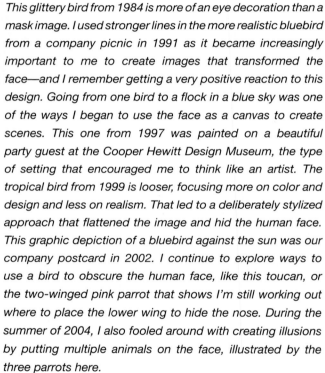

1999

2006

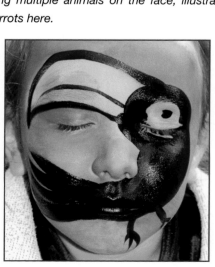

2002

2002

These two bird designs, painted at events in 2005, exemplify the inspiration I've found in the work of contemporary masters of this art. Seeing the beautiful and precise use of linework in classes with the master instructors at the Face and Body Art International Conventions has led me to challenge myself to improve my own brush work and incorporate more sophisticated linework within my design style.

Face by Miguel

Hat by
Wacky Wendy

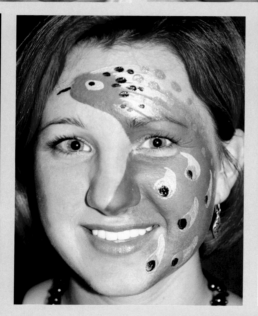

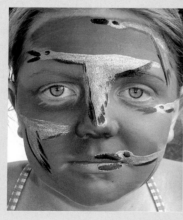

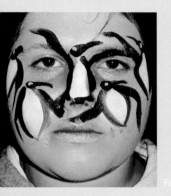

The Hen and the Dove

In a folktale from Africa, collected by a British official during the colonial period, the Hen and the Dove were great friends. Sitting together in a tree at the edge of the forest they made a plan. Food was scarce and both were hungry, so each promised to search for food and return with it to share with the other. The Dove flew off into the woods. The Hen decided she would go into the village of Man.

After some days the Dove returned to the tree, having found only some dried berries and a little wild grass. As the Hen was not waiting there, the Dove flew into the village of Man to look for her friend. She found her in the yard behind the house of Man and landed on a tree branch above.

"Friend, friend," said the Hen, "I am so glad you came. I have found food, more food than we've ever had before. Every day the Man puts it in his yard for me and I can eat as much as I like."

"Do you stay here in his yard?", asked the Dove.

"Yes," said the Hen, "for he wants me to be safe."

"And why has he put a string around your neck which is tied to his house post?" asked the Dove. "He cares for me very much," said the Hen. "I am so valuable that he doesn't want to lose me. Friend, I am sure that Man would care for you and feed you as well. Come back tomorrow and we will ask him."

The Dove flew away to the tree at the edge of the forest for the night.

The next day, when she returned to the village of Man, the Hen was not in the yard. The string that had been tied around its neck was lying there empty. When the Dog that belonged to Man walked into the yard the Dove asked, "Where is my friend the Hen?"

"My master said she ate so well that she had gotten fat enough," said the Dog, and he walked back into the house.

The Dove looked through the window and saw a large pot on the stove, cooking. The Dove knew that she did not want to be so valuable that she too would be cared for so.

The Dove flew away from the village of Man, back into the forest to search for berries and grasses, certain that it was better to fly free, even if you must struggle to live.

Face by Maria

Birds fly free...

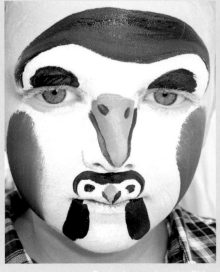

Design by my daughter Chloe

An alligator from around Halloween of 1995, in a photograph which has remained a favorite of mine for the feeling of menace the face evokes, despite the quick and sloppy execution. Bending the shape of the mouth as it went up the cheeks worked for me as a way to create the foreshortening necessary to depict an alligator's long mouth.

9 Snakes Dragons & Things

with Teeth

"You do a lot of boy designs," said a participant after a class in which I lined up volunteers and painted them in a set of our typical animal faces. She was referring to the number of tigers, dragons and snake faces I'd included. It was a compliment, as she thought boy designs are harder to come by. On the other hand, you might be surprised by how many little girls want to be made scary (and I do take a bit of pleasure in the discomfort of some parents when their little princess asks to become a snake).

In the theatre they say that everyone wants to play the villain. It's more fun than the hero. You get to chew up the scenery and cross the lines of decency. If you're lucky, you may have a glorious death scene—from which you get to come back to life. In the movies, of course, the bad guys always get the best makeup.

That same extravagance of style applies to face and mask art. You have so much to play with when you are going for spooky or powerful faces. There's inspiration in myriad masks depicting supernatural monsters and demons, and many examples of body art intended to make the wearer frightening to an enemy in combat or competition. In traditional cultures, the mask maker or body artist functioned

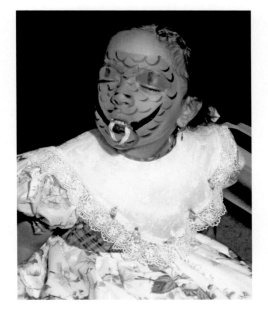

in part as a gate keeper to the spirit world. Their skill would allow supernatural figures to come to life in rituals and they might also be charged with disguising and protecting the shamans during their spirit journeys. This is exemplified by the survival of Halloween in our modern culture as the last vestige of fundamental traditions of transformational makeup in which you want to make yourself as spooky as the things you imagine are out there on a night when the door to the other world is open.

We humans like to depict ourselves as powerful, dangerous beings. At an event, offering kids the chance to become dangerous looking may help the recalcitrant decide to get themselves painted. Powerful animals also make powerful faces. Especially popular are things with teeth.

I am always willing to make someone look frightening. It's a primal function of facepainting to give the wearer access to attributes that are beyond their normal lives. And I think it is healthy for kids to becomes snakes, monsters and such, for if you can become the thing that frightens you, you no longer need to be afraid.

The evil image that snakes currently have in U.S. society is not a universal one. In many cultures the snake is a symbol for renewal and rebirth, as they shed and renew their skin. Within shamanist beliefs the snake may be revered as a guide, for they know how to move underground through the caves and rock which are the gateway to the spirit world (see page 17 for the snake face of the shaman Cobroti.) From there, perhaps, came the snakes wrapped around the "caduceus" wand of Hermes, the messenger god of the Greeks, who touched it to the eyes of the dead to show them the way to Hades. The entwined snakes survive today in the logos of the medical profession, our modern guides through life and death. The nascent United States even chose the snake as our first national symbol on the original "Don't Tread On Me" flag.

To a facepainter the snake presents a truly iconic image. The sinuous curve that is their body shape is instantly recognizable even in the most simplified form. For me, as I've said before, their significant element is also clear: if it has fangs, it's a snake. Fangs signify the poison, the power and the danger of the snake. Add a forked tongue and snake eyes to be sure.

Within our style, we use the features of the face to paint masks that come alive. The eyelids can become snake eyes in a full face mask like a tiger, or one eye can be used, as in the previous bird designs, for a snake in profile. However, as the significant features

of a snake involve its mouth, you have a third and very effective option of using the wearer's mouth, in many different ways, as the mouth of the snake.

Here's one of my favorite snake faces and it doesn't have fangs at all! I guess it's the exception that proves the rule. Or maybe it's a happy snake. We used this photo for one of our promotional postcards. I like it because the blue streak in the background matches her eyes. I also like the checkerboard background pattern that I quickly added with a 3/4" flat brush.

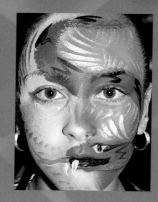   

The Mouth Snake:

An approach to painting a face when the goal is to put an image of an animal on the face, rather than turning the face into a mask of the animal.

BACKGROUND   When I am painting an image within a background such as this mouth snake (or a bird against a blue sky, a tiger leaping through a jungle, etc.) I like to start with the background. Block in one or two colors with a sponge leaving skin exposed where you will put in the main image. The shape of the bare skin you leave lets you see how the image will work with the structure of the face.

IMAGE   Add the snake with a sponge, creating a more precise shape and placement than that initial bare area. The face of the snake can work in profile across the mouth or facing forward as it does here. I use round, soft craft sponges which I pinch with my fingers to control the width and shape of the line of makeup they apply. It's like using a fat brush, but a sponge puts the makeup on faster and thinner, which let's you work on top of it better. Here, I also used a sponge to put the yellow eyes and stippled yellow for the belly on the snake—and extra yellow eyes on the person's eyelids just because snake eyes look cool.

For the boldest effect, use contrasting colors for the image and the background (like this green snake on a red background) or, since snakes are sneaky and often well hidden, use more similar colors (like green on blue) and less defined edges to let the snake blend into the background.

DEFINE   With my black brush I'll define the eyes and features of the snake. My snake eyes are more rounded than my cat eyes and, just as a cartoonist does, by controlling the shape and size of an animal's eyes you can create a range of expressions from cute to sinister.

I don't believe in outlining every image I put on a face. Full outlines can often be too strong and overpower the image. I use limited outlining to sculpt the image or to draw focus to part of the image, like the snake's head. I also left spaces in the black of the snake's mouth where I am going to put the fangs and tongue so I don't have to put those bright colors over wet black makeup.

DECORATE   When I am working quickly, I'm very economical with the number of colors I use. The same brush loads of black, red or white makeup I use for the outlines, tongue and fangs will be used to put some patterning over the snake and also to add some decorative elements to the background. These might be echoes of the snake's pattern or something like pairs of white lines evoking extra fangs to emphasize how poisonous it is.

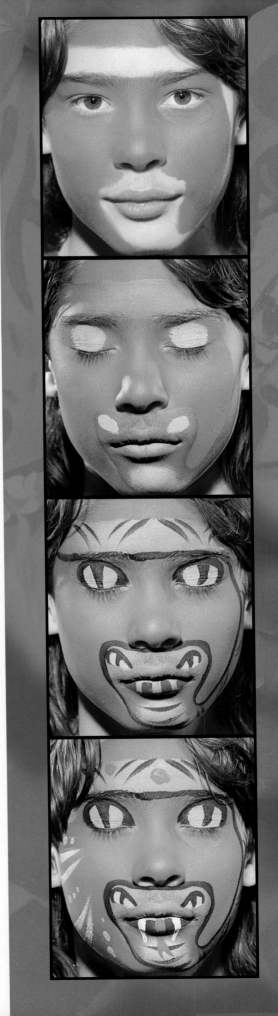

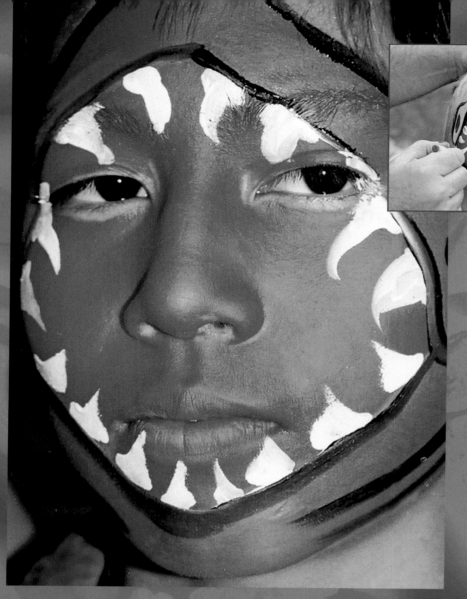

This is one of the best ideas I have ever stolen, and I can't figure out exactly where I got it from. It's such a dynamic mask image that I must have seen it somewhere, maybe as a young artist gleaning images in a book or museum with no knowledge of how I might one day use them. The idea is similar to the helmet mask examples from Chapter 6, but it's not really a helmet. There are also many examples of Northwest Coast Indian masks with faces depicted inside the mouth of a sea monster or killer whale, so I might have gotten the initial inspiration there.

It's the face I use to tell one of my favorite folktales, "Punia and the King of the Sharks," about a boy who allows himself to be swallowed by a shark so that he can kill it from the inside. It's a face that really tells the story, as you see both the boy's face and the shark's mouth simultaneously. It's also a great face for showing off at an event—for getting older kids, for example, to realize that what you are doing is not just for the little ones.

The Shark Mouth

From a Mask to a Face

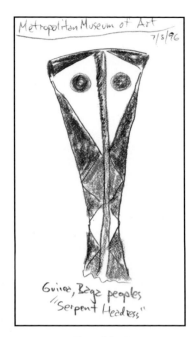

Baga Mask

In world cultures, the same designs that are used on faces are sometimes made into the more permanent object of a mask. The swirling patterns of Sepik Valley faces from Papua New Guinea become the painted designs on masks to represent a person after their death. The Maori would carve their facial moko into wooden sculptures with a similar purpose. Portrait masks of the Pacific Northwest Coast Indian cultures, and of many cultures around the world, include facepainting designs as a way to identify an individual. Thus, masks can be a direct source for faces, though there is usually a need to alter or translate the design.

Here's a sketch of that four-foot-tall wooden snake mask of the Baga people of Guinea, Africa, which I mentioned in Chapter 4. Seeing this mask got me to try using triangular shapes over the eyes for a snake, as in the top two faces on the left from zoo events in 1998 and '99, but there were several steps until I got to the face I like today.

Nuba Face Design

I knew snakes might have triangular patterns, or diamonds, on their bodies like the diamond-back rattle snake. To put them over the eyes as in the African mask might be an example of how significant animal signs are moved from the body onto the face in mask making. Than I saw the Gaboon viper in the Congo exhibit at the Bronx Zoo which had a line down the middle of its face and two black triangles right over its eyes like a mask. We'd also found the analytical sketches of basic face patterns of the Nuba that summer (see pages 16 and 60-63) which included dramatic designs which used triangles to give the focus to the eyes. So I followed those images and made this mask simpler to become one of my favorite spooky snake types, as in the bottom two examples on the left. Like the shark face, it lets people know you take your facepainting seriously.

The Gaboon Viper — watercolor by Naoko

This face came from a mask inspired by an Aztec ritual.

While painting at a festival in Mexico (see page 111), I found the book *Mexican Masks* by Donald Bush Cordy (1980) on my friend Sigfrido's bookshelves. It included many examples of wooden snake masks. A few depicted a human face with fangs, holding a snake in its mouth. The author suggested that these were masks intended to represent an older Aztec ritual, a competitive dance in which the dancers would pick up a live snake with their mouths. The winner was the first one to swallow the snake.

This is an example of a traditional function of masks to represent or replace ritual acts. Masks are also used at times to formalize or replace transformations originally achieved through body art. As a facepainter, I work in the other direction, taking the formal image of a mask and bringing it back to life on a face.

109

Fiery Dragons

I like to make my dragons dark, set against a fiery background. They make a great, iconic image in black silhouette against reds, oranges and golds. Use an eye for the dragon's eye, or the mouth for a fire-breathing mouth, or place the dragon's head on the forehead with dark wings making a mask across the eyes. Take advantage of the inherent shapes on the face for the curving body and the thrusting claws. Add minimal details like a yellow underbelly, golden scales or day-glo orange swirls for the fire.

Dragons are not real animals, so why try to make them realistic? They are primal symbols of majesty and power. They are uncontrollable. Their representational image should be equally bold and wild. Too much detail can tame a dragon. Keep your dragons loose and free, dominating the face.

Painting at the Cervantino

This dragon face has become a touchstone for me as to how much can be achieved by how little. One line in the right place is worth a dozen details. Capturing the correct gesture in your lines and shapes is what makes a design effective.

For four days we were part of the 2001 Festival International Cervantino, scheduled as one of many free outdoor performances at this gathering of dozens of theatre, music and dance companies from around the world. Janet and I were painting in a beautiful plaza in the heart of Guanajuato, Mexico, the host city. By the second day we had a long line of people waiting as we arrived to set up. Although everyone was patient and appreciative, we wanted to paint as many people each day as possible.

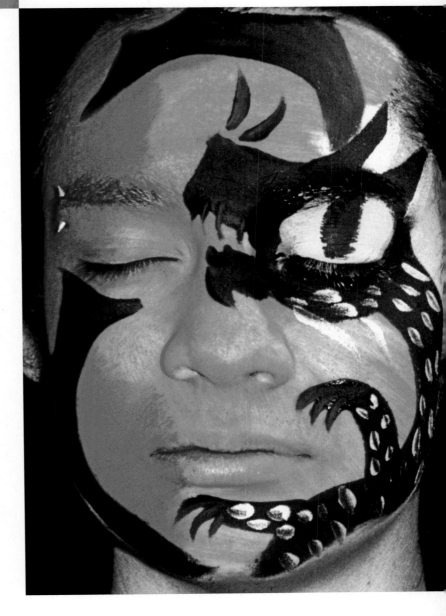

You can't hurry up in order to paint fast. You need instead to be more economical with your design and technique. The black brush I used for this dragon was a fat one. I sometimes put all the fine brushes away on the days when the lines are long.

The vibrant colors in the arts and masks of Mexico were also telling us to be extra bold as we painted. The majority of the people we painted were adults, theatre and art students from around Mexico, so the designs we used were strong.

After hard days of painting we went out at night to see wonderful performances in the streets and theatres of Guanajuato. Everywhere we went we saw painted faces in the audiences and knew we had succeeded in bringing our art of transformation to the Cervantino.

Janet painting a Snake Face

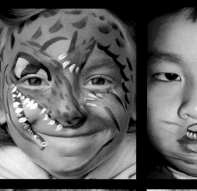

Bodypainting by Maria

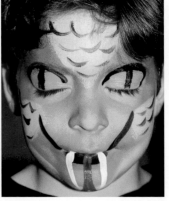

The enigmatic snake has served me as a vehicle for demonstrating for young audiences how an animal mask might be made realistic or represented through symbols and shapes in a tribal style, as in this photo from an early version of my "Heads & Tales" storytelling show.

In pictorial representations, the simple form of the snake's body allows for the greatest variety of possible placements on the face. The eye, mouth, forehead or nose all work for a snake's head, and then just wrap the body around anywhere you will. In representational terms, dragons are snakes with teeth and claws. They have fewer curves, but you get that fire to play with. Alligators are less sinuous still, and their representation needs to feature their mouth and all those lovely teeth.

Snakes, Dragons & Things With Teeth   113

The Tiger Gets Loose

10
Matisse's Cat
designing a new cat face

faces; later, with the Congo event, we brought cultural imagery into the company style. It's never like the periods that canvas painters go through, where every painting is within a certain style—such as the Cubist or Blue periods of Picasso. It's more like a musician who keeps adding new songs to the favorites that make up his repertoire. Facepainting is wonderful in how it lets you present great variety even within one event.

With cultural masks an established part of our repertoire, we began exploring in another direction, using the structure of the human face pictorially rather than as a mask. I took two approaches to find interesting ways to put two dimensional imagery over the curves and shapes of a face: one, hiding the facial features so that the painted image becomes dominant, creating a visual illusion; two, forgetting it's a face and treating it more purely as a curved surface to create a painted canvas which happens to be looking at you.

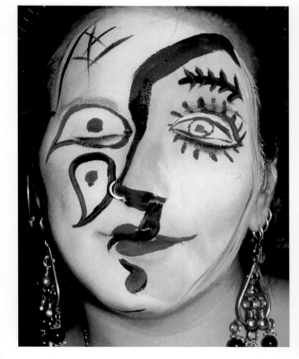

Walk through an art museum, from ancient to modern art, and imagine how each of those artists might paint a face. From that perspective, there is no one "right way" to paint a face. There are always other possibilities, other approaches to try.

As the artistic director of a facepainting company, it is my job to push ahead, to find new directions to explore. Most of our artists have their own careers in other media and bring their own skills and styles to what we do. I set standards and open doors. Sometimes I'll develop an idea that I want to show to them. Mostly I just set off in a new direction and know they will follow in their own way.

We learned that the Bronx Zoo would be opening their new Tiger Mountain exhibit in the Spring of 2003. That would mean many events devoted to tiger faces. So I needed some big cat designs to add new life into the mix of familiar tiger faces we were all using.

As I assembled this book, the photographs I reviewed record different conceptual approaches over the years. Once, my animal faces were as realistic as possible; for large events in the '90s there are simpler graphic designs to paint fast, full

I am certainly not inventing the wheel here. I see examples of these ideas in my own work from the past and better examples in the work of other body artists. You can also find some of these same facial illusions in places like Chinese Opera makeup. So when I say I am discovering things, it is in the personal sense. I am pushing my own understanding of these concepts and seeing what faces I can paint that are new for me. I am "squeezing the juice out of the lemon" as my friend and teacher Sigfrido would say. If you want to make face-painting your art, you have to work toward better ways to understand the face—and not just better ways to paint the same faces. That is the vehicle for continuing creativity.

Determining how an image can fit onto the features of a face is the process I call "placement," and I think it is the essential step in designing new and different faces.

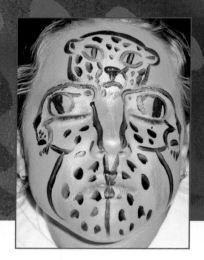

For the summer of Tiger Mountain this "face as a canvas" approach became a way to generate new tiger designs. I began by collecting photos and drawings of big cats because it's a style dependent on imagery. I looked for action poses because I wanted to express the power of the animals in a way similar to the experience of seeing them up close in the new exhibit. From these images, I made sketches in my notebook to learn the essential lines and shapes of the animals in motion.

You don't need to learn how to paint every animal in every possible pose to be able to generate a variety of faces. Once you have practised a simple depiction of a growling tiger head in profile, for example, you can make multiple designs by placing it in different positions on the face. You can enlarge or reduce it. You can place it so that you use the person's eye as the tiger's eye, or their mouth as the tiger's mouth.

Determining how an image can fit onto the features of a face is the process I call "placement," and I think it is the essential step in designing new and different faces. Finding ways to make your imagery use the curves and features of the face turns an image into an effective, living mask.

I do this by sketching onto a simplified representation of a face using printed sheets of face ovals, with eyes, nose and mouth indicated. The first placement choice is whether to use or avoid the features of the face (Ex: Should the head of the leaping tiger be placed to use the person's eye as the tiger's, or should it go onto the open area of the forehead instead?) From there I try to place the rest of the image to take advantage of the face. The face has inherent lines and shapes (in the cheek bones and jaw line, for

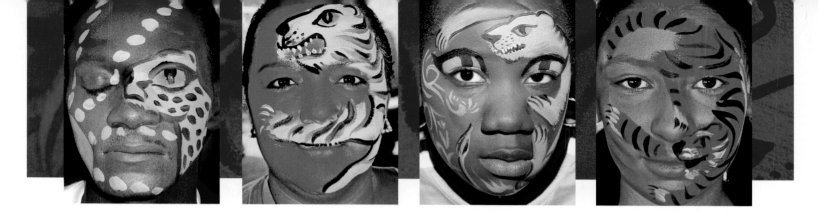

example), so it is like matching pieces of a jigsaw puzzle to see where your image fits onto the shapes of the face. How the design works as a painted mask is more important than the real image of the animal, so I will adjust and distort that image to better fit the features—which is also the case in tribal and mask art, as discussed in Chapters 1 and 2.

The human nose is especially tricky. The way it sticks out makes it difficult to paint designs that cross the nose because it warps them. My basic approach is to avoid the nose unless I am intentionally using it for something that thrusts forward from the image (like a claw coming forward). If a line of your design goes down the center of the nose, that can also hide it.

From four pages of notebook tiger sketches I generated about forty face oval designs. On some the placement of the imagery seemed natural, on others it seemed forced, but you can never be sure if a design will work until you try it on a face—or on twelve faces. So next I took my new face oval designs to events and tried them on people. I tried, adjusted and developed these designs on faces at our regular events.

A few words about this. Show your skills on some great faces throughout the day and it's ok to take chances on some

others. Out of the 50-200 faces I'll paint at an event, maybe 10-40 will be "risky" designs. As I keep saying, if you let the people you are painting know you are an artist doing art, most of them enjoy being part of a creative process.

The second design step is a dialog between me and the faces I paint. If a new design isn't quite right when I try it in the first hour of an event I'll try it again several times before the day is done. When possible, I take photos of faces that have taught me something—especially the successes, but also the failures. For example, it didn't work to put the white tiger's leg across the upper lip in the photo above, but I did like the expressive pose of the tiger's head and have reused that for other designs.

Ultimately it's the sponge and the brush that tell me the best way to place a design on a face as I can *feel* the shapes and lines that fit the face I'm painting. When I begin to see which ones work best I'll focus on and refine those designs, maybe by re-sketching them onto face ovals or sometimes by drawing corrections onto photographs of my faces. Throughout this dialog process my primary focus is on the form and placement of the image, but I'll also experiment with elements like color.

Faces by Naoko   *Face by Marge*   *Face by Christine*

From out of this process I wound up with maybe a half dozen new tiger designs that joined my repertoire and maybe ten more I am still developing. For the zoo events I gave my artists copies of my notebook sketches, a set of the more successful face oval designs and showed them photographs of some of the better faces. In our company structure I do the bulk of the research and development, and

Face by Naoko

they get to take what I've discovered and make it their own. From their re-inventions I'll get more ideas, as we each are inspired by the faces of our fellow artists. The explorations I was making with putting big cats across the forehead, for example, led Naoko into a wonderful series of relaxed looking cats lounging on top of people's faces and this inventive placement of a paw down the nose.

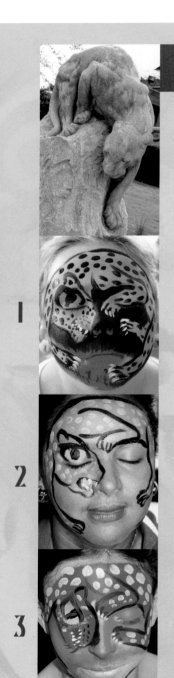

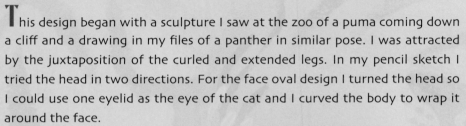

Developing The Forehead Cat Design

This design began with a sculpture I saw at the zoo of a puma coming down a cliff and a drawing in my files of a panther in similar pose. I was attracted by the juxtaposition of the curled and extended legs. In my pencil sketch I tried the head in two directions. For the face oval design I turned the head so I could use one eyelid as the eye of the cat and I curved the body to wrap it around the face.

The photographs here show how I varied the placement as I explored what this design looks like on a face. In an early attempt (1) I used black to blank out the human face (which was effective but time consuming), and made the mistake of putting the bent front leg right on the eyelid (which didn't look good when the eye was open.) Later that day, I found that the bent leg looks best right on the eyebrow, framing the eye in concert with the back leg painted on the cheekbone (2).

A deeper understanding came when I used my fattest black brush to paint this black panther (4) in the "large silhouette on a colorful background" style (see the Fiery Dragons page). I liked it enough that I showed it to the artists working with me that day. It reminded me of Matisse's papercut figures, like his blue swimmers, and thinking of his approach got me to loosen my hold on the realistic depiction of the cat image—I could adjust and stylize the legs to fit the face better. Stylizing also allowed me to work towards generating the meaning, the "feel," of a big cat as well as its appearance. In the subsequent tiger example (5) I enlarged the image so that it enveloped the face, as if the big cat has curled up to sleep.

Once you find the groove with a new design idea, you can adapt it to other subjects. This forehead cat concept became one of the crocodile faces in the gallery at the end of Chapter 9.

You really don't know what a design is capable of until you work with it on a face.

One personal discovery stands out from this process of designing a new cat face because it became a methodology that has led to many new faces. I call it the "loose" approach. Here I am working primarily with color and pattern to create an interesting face and then adding pieces of imagery as a defining feature.

Did you ever start painting a face before you knew how it would end? I imagine it's something we all do when working quickly with a line of waiting people. In Chapter 1, I describe a tribal approach that starts by dividing the face into shapes of color with signs and symbols added to make it into an animal.

The "loose" face is the same idea without the defined shapes and symbols. I start by putting colors on the face in an attractive way, taking advantage of the facial structure, with only a general sense of where the animal will go. Looking at that background I see where the cat, or pieces of the cat, can fit in and define it with limited features like a snarling head and claws. It's how you might see a tiger in the wild, a flash of color moving through the woods.

That led to playing with the patterns from the animals, like letting the stripes continue beyond the tiger or putting the spots onto the background instead of (or additionally) on the leopard. Using animal patterns in this way is also found in tribal body art.

Once the cats got "loose," I tried it with all sorts of animals like giraffes, zebras and fish, and it's helped me keep my birds and angels free. I've played with adding "loose" elements over another face, like the claws and head of a running cheetah on the more traditional cheetah mask face.

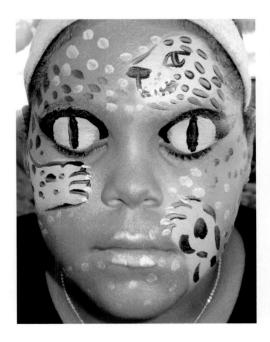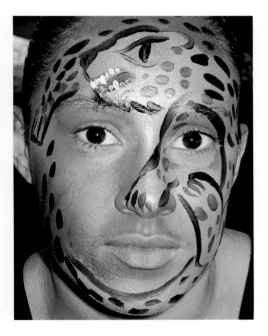

I've also started with tribal face divisions, like using green and ochre bands across the face, and then adding "loose" cheetah imagery. On people who ask for surprises, I sometimes put on a multi-colored background and then see what kind of animal wants to appear on top of it. I like that feeling of letting the face tell me what to do. It keeps me loose.

None of these "loose" faces has ever looked perfect to me because every time I paint one I look at it and see something else I could try—but it sure is a fun way to paint. This technical concept has become a creativity generator for me, with the same kind of exciting/frustrating results as when I'd try

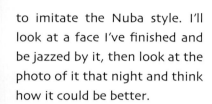

to imitate the Nuba style. I'll look at a face I've finished and be jazzed by it, then look at the photo of it that night and think how it could be better.

Let me be plain. Creativity and experimentation means you'll have failures as well as successes. Some ideas I've had for faces just didn't work out. I've also painted many bad or mediocre faces on the way to some really good designs.

So, why? Why take the risk?

Why not just paint the designs I know will always work?

The adventure involved in being creative is part of what keeps facepainting exciting for me, and for my audience. Finding new faces, and better ways to paint old faces, is as rewarding as the smiles on the faces we paint.

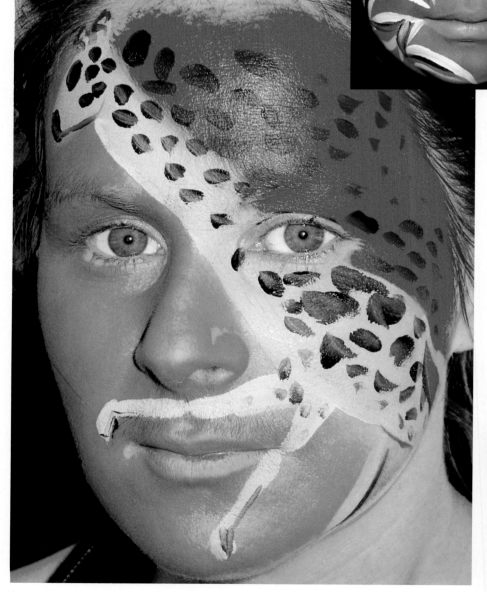

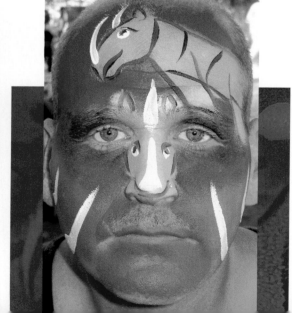

There is more to it. Creative risks are necessary for an artist's development. I have grown in my design and conceptual approach, and not just my skills, by challenging myself to move past my successful/comfortable faces. That is a key choice. You can progress by perfecting how you paint, but as an artist, you must work on expanding how you *think* about facepainting—especially how you think about your own facepainting. I'm not saying you have to follow my process and paint like me, or that you should paint like Matisse, for that matter. I'm saying that you need to establish a critical dialog with your own work. You need to care enough about your own work to see it as your art. Bring in inspirations, learn from teachers and colleagues, but, mostly, learn from yourself. The face you just painted, where can it lead you?

To think like this about the faces I paint has helped me enjoy facepainting for thirty years. I believe that it also adds to the enjoyment of the people I paint. Sure, sometimes a kid will be disappointed that I won't make them Spiderman, but usually I can still make them happy with whatever original design I turn them into, and, overall, I find that people are excited by the creativity they see, excited to wear the work of an artist who facepaints.

I don't paint a person's face just for them. I paint it for myself as well. I paint it for all the faces I will paint tomorrow and what it can

teach me about those faces. People lend me their face to be my canvas. That is a responsibility I take seriously. I strive to keep developing my art—to transform myself as I transform them.

In a major Matisse retrospective at the Museum of Modern Art in 1992, his *Large Reclining Nude* of 1935 was exhibited alongside photographs of the twenty different versions it went through as he painted and repainted the canvas from May through October until he got the version he was willing to exhibit.

Matisse made art right up until the end of his life, and it was only towards the end, he said, that he finally found the courage to use color the way he always wanted to.

It must be the plague of all artists if even the masters like Matisse were never satisfied with their work. Every time I look at a face I think, I feel, there has to be a way to do better. If I don't keep trying new ideas I'll never find out.

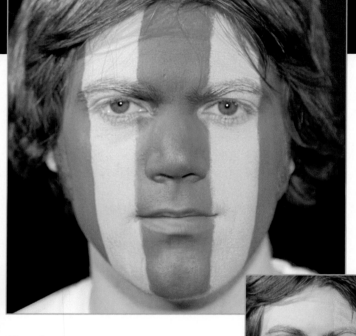

One Line

The first function of transformational makeup is to disguise who you are. Within cultures that use it most profoundly, the goal is beyond disguising individual personality. The goal is to disguise your human appearance entirely.

The quickest way to make a face appear nonhuman is to put a hard line on it. A line seems unnatural, because the human face is soft and curved.

Emphasize the line by using it to divide the face with two colors and you have that amazing half and half design we've all seen in both tribal and pop culture. It's a face design we are comfortable with—and not just from an old Star Trek episode. It's in our bones. Though familiar, it makes the face unnatural, in disguise, without human identity. When the Simbu people of Papua New Guinea paint their full bodies half white and half black the visual effect is the essence of transformational makeup: they are all alike, but we don't know what they are. They have established a tribal identity different from their individual personas.

Stripes

With a single line down the center of the face, the human identity is removed. Placing two vertical lines over the eyes achieves a very different effect as the focus is now directed to the eyes. The identity is gone and a new one appears. It's an identity that the wearer of the mask is in control of because we have to look at their eyes. When you complete this face with a contrasting color you have another basic tribal pattern: vertical stripes aligned over the eyes.

In both fashion and theatrical makeup you want to direct the attention to the eyes. As an acting student I was taught to use my eyes to hold the audience's attention and to let them know what my character was thinking. To know someone, to see who they truly are, you look into their eyes. They are the window to the soul.

In facepainting, using the eyes brings the painted mask to life, as in the cat faces with eyes painted on the eyelids. More than a parlor trick, it gives the wearers control over a mask they change whenever they open or close their eyes.

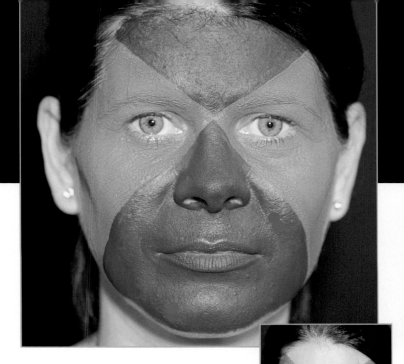

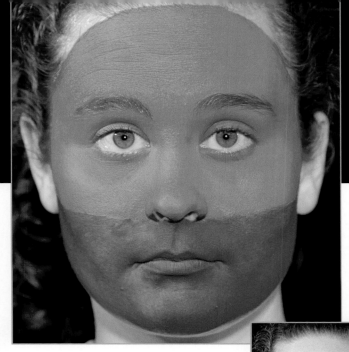

Shapes

In addition to lines and stripes you can alter and divide the face with geometric shapes. In his analysis of the "underlying raison d'être" for all tribal body painting, Michel Thévoz states: "the skin decoration is functionally designed to dehumanize, depersonalize,...to baffle identification. That is why...it makes play with anti-natural elements such as straight lines, triangles, circles and all rigid geometric figures which stand in conspicuous contrast with the mobility of facial features [and] the organic curves of muscles." While the immediate effect of the "anti-natural" skin decoration is to disguise the individual human identity, it simultaneously marks the wearer as a social being, a member of the social structure from which the significance of the body art is derived.

An especially effective use of hard geometric shapes over the curves of the face is to place two triangles as a mask over the eyes. The face is thus starkly divided into quarters which meet in the center at a single point. Not only are the eyes given a powerful framing device, the triangles act like arrows, drawing the viewer's complete attention into the mask through that one focal point right between the eyes.

Although this essential form is also the basis of the beautiful butterfly it works particularly well for designs that give power to the wearer. I think of it as a tribal superhero mask.

The Most Basic Mask of All

If a line is the primal facepainting element and the eyes our most important feature, then a line across the eyes is the most basic mask. And it's very effective. A stripe defining/disguising the eyes is found in face art around the world, from the primitive to high fashion.

If you want to disguise someone you cover his or her eyes. And we know it works, because no one ever realized that Robin was really the ward of millionaire Bruce Wayne.

A line across the eyes leads us to the top and bottom division of the face with a horizontal line that is found in tribal facepainting. Franz Boas points out that straight horizontal lines are rare in nature. They appear only in places such as the horizon formed by a body of water. Therefore, being able to make a horizontal line in art indicates a technical mastery beyond just imitating nature.

This line is thus a sign of civilization, and that returns us to the fundamental reasons for body art. More than a disguise, it is a way through art to establish our identity as part of society, to reveal what being human means and to prove our self-awareness.

We are part of the world of nature and we are more. With the power to transform ourselves, we are supernatural. In a painted face, we are all superheroes.

123

Two Lizards on Four Faces

Now that we have four faces in their transformational disguise, let's use them to tell a story.

Once there were two lizards who lived at the top of a tree in the forest. They were very happy, with plenty of bugs to eat and a very nice view.

One night—one terrible night—the wind began to blow, and their tree began to shake.

"Help! Help!" cried the lizards, "Our house is shaking! Our house is shaking!"

Then things got even worse. They heard a loud "crack!" as their tree broke in two, and down fell the lizards to the dark forest below.

"Help! Help!," cried the lizards, on the dark forest floor, "Our house is destroyed! Our house is destroyed!"

These are the two lizards falling down out of the tree.

"I can help you," said a deep voice. The lizards looked into the dark to see two eyes looking back at them as a long snake slithered out of the forest.

"I have a house you can come to," said the snake, "just climb onto my back and I'll take you there."

The lizards thanked the snake as they climbed onto his back, but they just had to ask, "Is it a nice house? Is it up in a tree like ours?"

"Well," said the snake as he slithered away, "it's actually very long and dark, and deep underground—and I'm taking you there for my dinner."

"Help! Help!" cried the lizards.

Things could not get any worse.

This is the face of the snake that wants to eat the lizards that fell down out of the tree.

Oh, the poor lizards, what could they do? Their house was destroyed, and now the snake wanted to eat them.

Just then they heard the sound of flapping wings as a bird—a tropical bird—flew down from the dark sky and snatched them off of the snake's back.

As the bird flew off with the lizards in its claws, they thanked it for saving them and told the bird that their house was destroyed.

"I have a house you can come to," said the bird as it flew through the dark night.

The lizards had to ask, "Is it a nice house? Is it up in a tree like ours?"

"Yes," said the bird, "it's a very nice house right at the top of a tree, and I have two little baby birds there who are very hungry."

"Help! Help! Help!" yelled the lizards.

Things could not possibly get any worse.

This is the bird who took from the snake the lizards that fell down out of the tree.

"Help! Help! Help!" the lizards yelled and yelled.

They made such a racket that the tropical bird decided that even a good meal was not worth all this noise so it let go of the lizards, and again they found themselves falling down through the dark.

Surely, this was the worst thing yet!

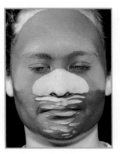

But even the darkest night has a dawn that follows.

That bird had flown so far from the forest that the falling lizards came down right onto the top of a palm tree, on a remote desert island.

As the sun rose they saw they were alone, with no snakes or birds to bother them. There were plenty of bugs to eat and a very nice ocean view.

So these are the lizards who lived in a tree on a tropical island, happy ever after.

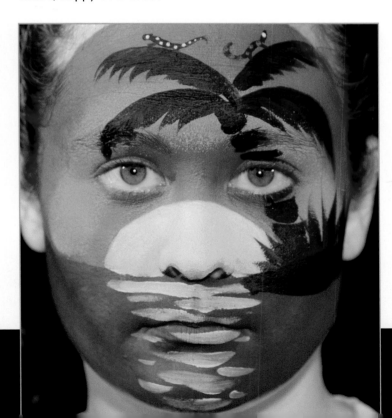

Throughout the process of writing this book—over a little more than a year's worth of events and painted faces—I have been thinking deeply about this art that is so often dismissed as a mere party entertainment. Setting aside the irony in that dismissal, given that face and body painting may have been the origin of art, I can confidently say that facepainting is an art if you choose to make it one when you paint a face. The canvas is alive, but it is still a canvas. Facepainting is an entertainment, but so are many arts.

Most of the people you paint do not expect you to be an artist and might pay the same for you to be at their kid's party whether you are an artist or not. So it is up to you, the facepainter. It is how you choose to approach each face that is the determining factor.

The adventure begins with the questions you ask yourself as you paint the face before you: where can this face lead me? What did I learn from the last face I painted?

With a creative approach, each face can offer an opportunity to explore. Each person who sits before you can be a new inspiration. Why should facepainting be just another job when it can be your art instead?

All of that deep thinking also meant that the past year's gigs lost a little of their joy at times as I found myself thinking too much about how, why and what I was painting while I was painting. Once the bulk of the text

and photography was complete I experienced a wonderfully renewed sense of enthusiasm and found myself having as much fun as I ever have had painting faces.

It is remarkable how enjoyable facepainting remains for me because, for a fun act that makes people smile, too often you have to do it in difficult settings with too many little faces to paint in too little time, and then there's the occasional unenlightened clients telling you how or what to paint. Yet it's the kind of job you might keep doing after you win the lottery. (Though you'd probably hire a roadie to carry all the makeup you'd buy).

What's not surprising is that it remains an adventure as an art form and as an exciting way to make a living. Facepainting is much too fun for me to want to let it get boring and that's why I keep looking for ways to bring inspiration into my work. It's led me to a world of faces, masks and traditional concepts that have profoundly enriched the adventure. And, as the omissions from these pages attest, there are still so many places for me to explore, such as the masks of Bali or the Aboriginal rock art and bodypainting of Australia. I have a lot of new faces yet to paint.

Each person who sits before you can be a new inspiration.

When we started doing special event weekends at the Bronx Zoo, I knew it was the ideal gig for artists who facepaint. For twelve years we were hired to paint free faces for the public as a promotional attraction on six to ten weekends a summer. I also knew that such a perfect situation wouldn't last forever.

In 2005 the zoo asked us to open a concession and be there on a daily basis instead. Keeping within our company's artistic goals, we set up a concession in which we post a list of animals to choose from rather than photos of how the faces should look, so each artist still gets to be creative (though we are getting asked to do more tigers and butterflies than we'd wish). The transition has been successful, but I do miss the halcyon summer days there of free facepainting for the masses when the artist's only concern was to paint amazing and creative faces... Well, "halcyon" is not the right word, because that describes a peaceful period (brought about by the halcyon bird that can calm winds and waters) and facepainting with long lines is not to be described as peaceful. Blissful, perhaps, but not peaceful.

We are still doing select special events at the zoo such as this past weekend's "Boo at the Zoo" with hundreds of adults and children getting painted for free. Some of the faces were familiar, as patrons tell us that coming to the zoo to be painted has become part of their family tradition. In most of the families some of the adults got painted, including some playful grandparents, and I can't say whether seeing them join in makes their kids or my artists more happy. We love to paint during the Halloween season and this year we put in an extra effort to

make all of our events a creative adventure. Rather than asking people what they wanted to be, we asked them how they wanted their face to make them feel, using key words such as dangerous, playful or tricky. Then the artist would translate that word into a concrete idea that became the basis for their painted face. Each key word itself was used to generate creativity and variety, as a word like "tricky" might one time become a tricky animal such as a raccoon, another time it might be a trickster character from world masks like the Chinese Opera monkey king, or it might inspire a tricky way to turn a face into an optical illusion. My goal was to let each artist feel the freedom to paint the faces that they wanted to paint, faces that they knew were spectacular, while fulfilling the traditional function of the mask maker to give the wearer an opportunity to experience a new identity. We had a great deal of fun painting like this, the people we painted were all smiling when they looked in the mirror to see what they'd become, and I am certain that the crowds that came through our tent were very well entertained.

Having figured out at the zoo how to present our facepainting as an art, using cultural inspirations and a creative approach, we have found that this act plays on the road. At the Darien Youth Arts Expo, for example, we painted World Masks on kids and their parents to fit an international theme. For the past few years at Albany First Night the people lined up for an hour and we never asked them what they want to be—everyone got a surprise. Marge and I were painting at a wedding recently, turning the kids mostly into butterflies and the like, and once we started doing a few tribal and mask faces many of the adults joined in. You can do serious art at all sorts of fun events.

This summer, Miguel came along to help me paint the audience after my *Transformation! Show* at a library. It was a show in which I did an old story with new faces, having been inspired by seeing Nathalie Simrad painting multiple faces simultaneously at the 2006 FABAI Convention the previous weekend. After the show, we were asking people for a favorite color so we could pick their animal and surprise them—to avoid having everyone choose the same animals I'd told stories about, as people tend to ask for the

things they've seen. We'd finished the kids and were painting some adults and staff. I got to my last face, a library page, and called Miguel over to show him an idea I'd been playing with for painting polar bears. Over a swirling blue background, I paint a partial outline of the polar bears with liquid white, then with my sponge I pull the white into the form of the polar bears, blending it slightly into the blue background to make polar bears with soft blue shadings and white highlights, as in the photo here from a different event. This time I was doing it on pink and purple, because the girl asked for those colors—it's nice when your canvas gives you new ideas, because shadowy white polar bears look fine on pink and purple. The library page we'd already painted was watching and she said to her friend, "Hey, how come you get to be the one he experiments on?" She was disappointed that it wasn't her.

We are modern practitioners of a most ancient art. Thought of in those terms it shouldn't be surprising that you can take the fun act of painting someone's face seriously. Any facepaint, even cheek art, is more than just a decoration. It is an alteration of a person's image in the eyes of all those who view them. The subjective experience of the person you paint doesn't end when they look into the mirror, it continues through the reactions of everyone who sees their painted face. Painting a face is giving the wearer a new identity, however temporary.

By changing how the world perceives them, you will also alter their perception of the world and of themselves. With a little facepaint we offer an experiential answer to the fundamental human question: *who are we?*

Through our art, we are anything we can imagine ourselves to be—we are the stuff of our dreams.

Transcending our own desire to be creative and how much we enjoy making facepainting into a show is the effect that this has on the people we paint. By presenting our facepainting as a traditional art we take advantage of the power in that tradition. By adding context and meaning to our faces we encourage the wearer to *feel* transformed. By surprising people with the face we put on them we give them an opportunity to ex-

perience an identity beyond themselves. Their willingness to join in this artistic process, to let us be creative, makes them an active part of the transformation. Through the art of the facepainter, that little bit of surrender sets the wearer free.

The adventure continues...and we still have to work. These are some of the faces I enjoyed painting at gigs from June through October of 2006 as the book art was getting readied for the printer.

129

Appendix

foto by Michael Mella

acknowledgments

I am deeply indebted to the following three people, without them there would be no book:

Joe Korts, of Kryolan, who initiated this book project and encouraged me to make it my own.

Christa Agostino for making the book itself into a work of her art and for her invaluable editorial work.

My brother Tom for rescuing my unprofessional and badly lit event photographs—help I never had to ask for.

Special thanks also to:

Michael Benson for his editorial assistance.

Rick Erickson and Dale Fuller for timely advice.

Naoko Oshima for her watercolor.

And to Lorraine Zeller-Agostino, my wife and facepainting partner, for doing everything else while I did this.

After thirty years it was time to share what I've discovered before the arm falls off and the brushes and sponges all wear out.

Thank you to the many clients and venues that in effect are the patrons of our art; to Lauren Roth, Michael Bongar, David Levitan and all of the event producers who appreciate our approach and get us into great gigs; and to the wonderful events that have hosted us such as the St. Francis Day Fair, Socrates Sculpture Park, NYC Parks and Recreation, and the cities of Albany, NY and Westport, CT.

Thank you to Marcela Murad and Cynthia Keeler for the FABAI Conventions and all that they do.

Thank you to Wolfram Langer and the Kryolan company, both for agreeing to publish this book, and for making Aquacolors, the first great face and body paints (and, in my opinion, still the best).

And to the Alcone Company for being such a friendly and supportive place to get our makeup.

The Wildlife Conservation Society has allowed us to bring our art to tens of thousands of people each year at the Bronx Zoo, NY Aquarium and Prospect Park Zoo, due, in large part, to the unqualified support of our work by Rachel Libretti, Director of Event Marketing. I can't imagine a better person to work for than Rachel, who has always allowed us to present our facepainting as an art. Thank you, Rachel.

By letting people feel a connection to the animals they become when we paint their faces, I hope we have contributed to the Society's mission of preserving the world of Nature.

the photographers

All the faces in this book have been washed off. For a facepainting artist, only the photographs survive beyond the initial live exhibit.

Many of the photographs in the book were taken by our company artists and our friends. Miguel, Sigfrido, Lorraine and Kate took some of the nicer photos of us in our tent at the Bronx Zoo. Some from the Cervantino Festival were by two helpful artists, Ophelia and Raul. Thank you to Jeremy and Chloe for photos of my shows.

Michael Mella provided photographs from the Congo summer and various corporate events.

Lorraine was the principal photographer for the studio sessions required for this project. We are indebted to Jack Cappon for lending us his equipment and expertise, and for taking the photographs of the Butterfly Girls with the assistance of his wife Shelly.

Thank you to our neighbor John Stahl for the gracious loan of his lens and for his photographs of the butterfly.

Most of the photos in the book are snapshots of people I painted at events. I take them right as I finish the face with the person still sitting in the chair before me—as you can tell by the light glinting on the wet makeup.

The thousands of photographs in my albums must only be a small percentage of all those taken by other photographers, the families and the friends of the people I paint. Thank you to all the people who have taken photographs of the faces that I and my colleagues have painted, so that they might live beyond their encounter with soap and water.

the people

My deepest thanks are owed to the tens of thousands of people who have lent me their face for my art.

I have noticed at events that anyone might line up for a balloon or party favor, but only some people choose to be facepainted. The people we paint give us control, however briefly, of their image in the world. Facepainting is not a passive art. It requires an act of surrender or openness on the part of the wearer and a taking of responsibility on the part of the artist.

Our *Transformation!* approach means that people don't know what they will look like until they see themselves in the mirror. Often they don't even know what they are going to become. I ask a lot of the people I paint, especially in my stage presentations: sit down, sit still, be quiet, close your eyes and when you open them you'll be... well, you won't know what you'll be until I explain it to you. And still they raise their hands to volunteer or line up to get painted. For so many people over the years to have given us that freedom means more to me than the compliments that all good facepainters are used to getting for the finished faces.

Thank you to the friends and colleagues who have served as my models over the years and have allowed me to experiment with designs too complicated for painting at public events. The featured models, past and present, who allowed me to take the extra time to paint some of the special faces and bodies for this project include: Jenn, Diane, Maria, Miguel, Christine, Monique, Jennifer, Noel, Naoko, Niru, Lizi, Zak, Jennifer Wilkinson, Anthony, Helena, Anya, Cassandra, Andyra, and, especially, my two beautiful children, Jeremy and Chloe. Perhaps the most surprising thing is that, having gone through the tedious process of the precision facepainting some designs require, followed by the even more tedious process of photographing their face, they all offered to do it again if I needed them (except for my kids).

Thank you to the hundreds of accidental models whose faces appear in this book. As I take my snapshots of the people I paint I ask if it's OK, and everyone says "yes". A few ask about how I use them, which might be on our displays or our web site, just for my own files, or now, in a book. It is the nature of facepainting that the identity of the individual in the photo is obscured, but you know who you are. If you see your picture in this book, drop me a line and tell me what you remember about being painted.

Without the canvas there is no painting. When the canvas is a living, breathing person then even the simple act of facepainting becomes profound.

a note about the facepainting

All the faces in the book were painted with a water-based makeup with sponges and brushes. The faces vary, but the application technique is fundamentally the same for all of us. We prefer Kryolan Aquacolors for the ease and flexibility of application that allows us to paint all the different types of faces we want, and to paint them quickly. And we love the brilliance and density of the colors.

As tempting as it is to go back and fix my mistakes and hasty brushstrokes, we have done very little photo retouching. At our public events we paint as many people as possible as quickly as we can and most of the faces in the book were painted in two or three minutes. My main focus is on the overall effect of the faces and how they transform both the individual and the event, so I've never been overly concerned with the small imprecisions (like the "painter's holidays" in which you miss a spot of skin when quickly sponging on a background color) that are more apparent in photographs than when looking at the living painted face—so we left all those glorious mistakes in. We've tried to get the colors to match the appearance of the painted face, and, in a few cases, we've had to correct an errant hair or a confusing highlight due to wet makeup.

On the whole, the facepainting is presented as is.

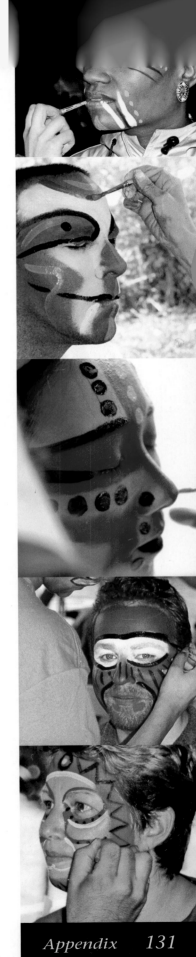

the company

The first face I painted was in 1976, as a young actor asked to help turn hundreds of my fellow high school students into clowns for a bicentennial parade. By the next summer, the members of our theater troupe had opened a facepainting concession at Adventureland Amusement Park on Long Island, NY. I haven't stopped painting faces since. (Why would I? It's too much fun).

In the eighties I began to look at facepainting differently—as an art. The art of transformation. In 1983 I was in LA, painting faces and bodies at Venice Beach. I joined with another performer and visual artist, Jennifer Green, to promote facepainting to museums and art shows as well as the usual gigs. Jenn's approach to a face was very different from mine. On the same day that I painted the classic Chinese Opera design on her for the photo on page 37, she turned me into abstract art.

When I returned to New York, I got a gig painting faces in the window of Unique Clothing right on Broadway in Greenwich Village and worked there on and off through the mid-'80s. It was facepainting as public entertainment. As was the case at both the amusement park and Venice Beach, I was painting more adults and teens than kids. I worked on ways to blend my theatrical approach and the Chinese Opera imagery with the punk styles people were wearing on the streets.

The extensive event industry in New York let me move from street fairs, where people paid for each face, to being hired for pri-

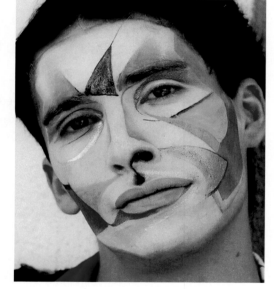

vate parties and corporate events. Sometimes I'd be able to bring along another artist who painted full faces, but most often there would be other freelance facepainters on these gigs with their own styles or just doing cheek art.

As the work became more steady and the events larger, I wanted to always work with a group of artists who approached this art like I did, to present facepainting as more than a cute diversion for little kids. That led in the '90s to the formation of the company, *Transformation! Facepainting*, and that was when facepainting really became fun.

Having a facepainting home like the Bronx Zoo over the past fourteen years has allowed us to maintain a company of very experienced artists. The current members of *Transformation! Facepainting*, roughly in the order in which they joined, are Lorraine Zeller-Agostino, Dennis Pettas, Michele Carlo, Danny Gosnell, Naoko Oshima, Roberta Halpern, Marge Gosnell-Qua, Jennifer Wade, Maria Pirone, Miguel Cossio, Sigfrido Aguilar, Janet Izzo, Laura Metzinger, Denise Lord, Nirupama Kumar, Christine Gregory, Zak Brown, Lizi Costache, Regina Russo and Phil Zirkuli. In this book full of my snapshots of my own faces, their work is vastly under-represented in proportion to their contribution to the success of our company.

The artists who find their way into our company tend to stay with us. It's so much fun and we like each other.

Before I had an organized troupe, I had friends to paint with. I'd get canvas painters I knew, like Wanda Boudreaux, to try face-painting. Wanda's from New Orleans, so we also got a chance to paint down there for Mardi Gras, and I have always felt that I learned as much from artists like Wanda as they learned from me.

Some of the other artists I've painted with along the way include Kate Cain Madsen (who began like me back at Adventureland and still paints with us when she's in town), Teddy Goldman, Anne Farmer, Diane Epstein, Suzanne Haring and her sisters, Jodi Levitan, Susan-Rachel Condon, Angela Izrailova, Miko and Claudia Reese, Jin Young Park, Luanne Dietrich, Erica Borillo and Therese Schorn. Some of these artists were with me as I first began to discover what I wanted to do with a face.

A facepainter is an artist who entertains, and entertainers get into the most interesting places. One day we may be painting at a party in the inner recesses of the New York Stock Exchange and the next day we're painting an endless line of kids in the Bronx for the Parks Department.

Just last summer, *Transformation! Facepainting* was hired by the Nature Conservancy for the Long Island Beach Festival. It was a wonderful event, right on the beach at Smiths Point Park. I got to tell stories and talk about nature and facepainting to the crowd strolling through the tent, and we got a chance to dip our toes in the ocean afterwards.

This is a wonderful business.

Usually for such events I'll give the artists a theme and maybe some source images like masks or sea life photos and they will invent their own faces. This time I tried something different. I gave to the three artists working with me (Naoko, Marge and Miguel), a set of 70 sea life faces I had sketched out for an earlier project at the New York Aquarium and asked them for that day to use my designs rather than their own. We told the crowd we were painting not to worry about what they wanted to be, that everyone would be surprised with a different sea life face.

As these three accomplished artists, who I have worked beside for years, began painting my face designs each took their own approach, brought their own style and vision, and none of the faces looked like I'd painted them. What a pleasure it was to work beside them.

For such artists to believe me when I tell them what I think is possible in this unconventional medium; for them to let me give them certain rules for painting on certain days; for colleagues to let me set a course for their creativity—this is all a very unexpected consequence of my decision to be a facepainter. To have a company of artists who want to do what I do amazes me.

bibliography

Bancroft-Hunt, Norman. *North American Indians*. London: Quintet Publishing, 1992.

Beckwith, Carol and Angela Fisher. *African Ceremonies: The Concise Edition*. New York: Harry N. Abrams, 2002.

Beckwith, Carol and Angela Fisher. *Faces of Africa: Thirty Years of Photography*. Washington, D.C.: National Geographic Society, 2004.

Boas, Franz. *Primitive Art*. New York: Dover Publications, 1955. (originally published in 1927, H. Aschelong and Co.).

Bodmer, Karl and Maximilian Prinz zu Wied. *The American Indian*. Cologne: Taschen, 2005. (reprinted from journals of 1839-1841).

Burenhult, Göran, ed. *Traditional People Today: The Illustrated History of Humanity, vol. 5*. McMahons Point, Australia: Weldon Owen Pty., 1994.

Camphausen, Rufus C. *Return of the Tribal: A Celebration of Body Adornment*. Rochester, Vermont: Park Street Press, 1997.

Chang, Isabelle C. *Chinese Fairy Tales*. New York: Schocken Books, 1968.

Chuang-Tsu, translated by Gia-Fu Feng and Jane English. *Inner Chapters*. New York: Vintage Books, 1974.

Clottes, Jean. "Rhinos, Lions and Bears (Oh, My!)" *Natural History*. (May 1995): 30-35.

Cordy, Donald Bush. *Mexican Masks*. Austin: University of Texas Press, 1980.

Delio, Michelle. *Tattoo: The Exotic Art of Skin Decoration*. New York: St. Martin Press, 1993.

Elderfield, John. *Henri Matisse: A Retrospective*. New York: The Museum of Modern Art, 1992.

Erdoes, Richard and Alfonso Ortiz, eds. *American Indian Myths and Legends*. New York: Pantheon Books, 1984.

Faris, James C. *Nuba Personal Art*. Toronto: University of Toronto Press, 1972.

Galeano, Eduardo. *Memory of Fire, Part One: Genesis*. New York: Pantheon Books, 1985.

Godwin, Peter. "Bushmen." *National Geographic*. (February 2001): 91-116.

Gröning, Karl. *Body Decoration: A World Survey of Body Art*. New York: Vendome Press, 1998.

Gudnason, Jessica Tan. *Chinese Opera*. New York: Abbeville Press, 2001.

Gurney, George and Therese Thau Heyman, eds. *George Catlin and His Indian Gallery*. Washington, D.C.: Smithsonian American Art Museum, 2002.

Kirk, Malcolm with essay by Andrew Strathern. *Man As Art: New Guinea*. San Francisco: Chronicle Books, 1993.

Lechuga, Ruth D. and Chloë Sayer. *Mask Arts of Mexico*. San Francisco: Chronicle Books, 1994.

Leiter, Samuel, ed. *Japanese Theater in the World*. New York: The Japan Society, 1997.

Lévi-Strauss, Claude. *The Way of the Masks*. Seattle: University of Washington Press, 1982.

Lewis-Williams, David. *The Mind in the Cave*. London: Thames & Hudson, 2002.

Lewis-Williams, David. "Paintings of the Spirit." *National Geographic* (February 2001): 118-125.

Littleton, C. Scott. *Mythology: The Illustrated Anthology of World Myth & Storytelling*. London: Duncan Baird Publishers, 2002.

Lommel, Andreas. *Prehistoric and Primitive Man*. New York: McGraw-Hill, 1966.

Macnair, Peter L., Robert Joseph and Bruce Grenville. *Down From the Shimmering Sky*. Vancouver: Douglas & McIntyre, 1998.

Malin, Edward. *A World of Faces: Masks of the Northwest Coast Indians*. Portland, Oregon: Timber Press, 1978.

Miller, Mark. "Maya Masterpiece Revealed at Bonampak." *National Geographic*, vol. 187, no. 2 (February 1995): 50-69.

Morita, Toshiro. *Kumadori*. Tokyo: JICC Co., 1985.

Nicholas, Anne. *The Art of the New Zealand Tattoo*. New York: Citadel Press, 1994.

Nunley, John W. and Cara McCarty. *Masks: Faces of Culture*. New York: Harry N. Abrams, 1999.

Packer, Craig and Jean Clottes. "When Lions Ruled France." *Natural History* (November 2000): 52-57.

Riefenstahl, Leni. *The People of Kau*. New York: St. Martin's Press, 1977.

Robley, H.G. *Maori Tattooing*. New York: Dover Publications, 2003. (originally published in 1896, Chapman and Hall).

Shankar, Ravi. *Kerala*. New Delhi: Roli Books, 2001.

Solis, Felipe, curator. *The Aztec Empire: Catalogue of the Exhibition*. New York: Guggenheim Museum Publications, 2004.

Spivey, Nigel. *How Art Made the World: A Journey to the Origins of Human Creativity*. New York: Basic Books, 2005.

Thévoz, Michel. *The Painted Body*. Geneva: Editions d'Art Albert Skira, 1984.

Tyler, Royall, ed. *Japanese Tales*. New York: Pantheon Books, 1987.

Wang-Ngai, Siu with Peter Lovrick. *Chinese Opera: Images and Stories*. Vancover: UBC Press, 1997.

Willet, Frank. *African Art: An Introduction, revised edition*. New York: Thames & Hudson, 1993.

Wiseman, Boris and Judy Groves. *Introducing Lévi-Strauss*. New York: Totem Books, 1998.

Wolfe, Art. *Tribes*. New York: Clarkson N. Potter, 1997.

——. "The Ageless Art of Chinese Opera." *Geo*, vol. 2 (December 1980).

thematic index

general index

Every face has its story…

Watakure, The Boy Who Loved Nature

…a South American Wonder Tale

Each of the parrots gave a feather to make a roof for his house like none had ever seen.

The frogs told him to look under the bed, and there he found the snake…

…the snake who was glad to help.

The spiders wove webs across the path to slow his enemies.

The crocodile came from the river to guard his house at night.